Contents

There is a hope...

It's been a strange year. What will the coming months bring? Sadness and suffering maybe – and these are familiar themes through the centuries of God's people, from Genesis to Revelation. And, of course, in our own times too. Yet always there are moments of joy – successes, new birth, times with family and friends. More than these, there is God's eternal story, which leads us on in our hope in Christ, to life where sin and suffering are no more. In this issue of *Daily Bread*, that hope of Christ threads through our readings, from ancient times to resurrection.

The book of Leviticus brings its challenges to contemporary readers. Yet, writer David Lawrence helps us to understand the old Law in the light of our hope in Christ. Praise God that *our* sin has been dealt with through his sacrifice! That golden thread leads us on through the prophets, where the God of mercy demonstrates his love and salvation through the words of Hosea and Jonah. And then, we come to the story of Christ himself, told through Luke's Gospel. We travel with his disciples to Jerusalem, the cross and resurrection.

Today, we walk that way of hope, remembering believers of the early church, facing our own challenges to faith, always looking forward to the day of his coming (1 Thessalonians 4:16–18).

As Ben Green reminds us in his series on Thessalonians, let's hold on to our faithful God, encouraging one another, building each other up in our hope in Christ: 'The one who calls you is faithful, and he will do it' (1 Thessalonians 5:24).

'Tricia and Emlyn Williams
Editors

Daily Bread toolbox

Tricia & Emlyn Williams worked with Scripture Union for many years. Emlyn led schools ministry, then worked with SU International. Tricia was also part of the schools team and later worked for SU Publishing, developing and writing Bible resources. In recent years Tricia has been researching and writing about faith and dementia. Now living in Norfolk, they both continue their writing, editing and talking-with-people ministries, and are involved in a local Anglican church.

WAY IN

This page introduces both the notes and the writer. It sets the scene and tells you what you need to know to get into each series.

A DAY'S NOTE

The notes for each day include five key elements: *Prepare*, *Read* (the Bible passage for the day), *Explore*, *Respond* and *Bible in a year.* These are intended to provide a helpful way of meeting God in his Word.

PREPARE

Prepare yourself to meet with God and pray that the Holy Spirit will help you to understand and respond to what you read.

READ

Read the Bible passage, taking time to absorb and simply enjoy it. A verse or two from the Bible text is usually included on each page, but it's important to read the whole passage.

EXPLORE

Explore the meaning of the passage, listening for what God may be saying to you. Before you read the comment, ask yourself: what is the main point of this passage? What is God showing me about himself or about my life? Is there a promise or a command, a warning or example to take special notice of?

RESPOND

Respond to what God has shown you in the passage in worship and pray for yourself and others. Decide how to share your discoveries with others.

BIBLE IN A YEAR

If your aim is to know God and his Word more deeply, why not follow this plan and read the whole Bible in one year?

Amazing Grace in 2023

It was John Newton's personal experience of God's goodness that led him to scribe 'Amazing Grace'* – 250 years on, James Taylor also knows what it is to have been lost and found. James' experience of God's wonderful love came through SU's Perranporth mission; now he leads a church in Taunton.

James grew up in Perranporth. His parents were not Christians, but his mother used to take him to Perranporth Mission because he was an only child and she thought he'd enjoy playing with other children.

James says, 'I went to the mission each summer from the age of three. When I was ten, the leaders gave me a youth Bible and a music tape by the Christian band Delirious?.'

James kept the Bible by his bed but didn't reach for it, as he struggled with reading. But the Delirious? tape later

*The cover for this quarter celebrates the 250th anniversary of the writing of 'Amazing Grace'.

proved to be a lifeline, as his life took a downward turn. James developed body dysmorphia, a mental health condition where he became obsessed with his appearance, which he felt was defective. By the time he was 11, he was starting to use drink and drugs as a means of escape. James did not go to the mission the following summer. He felt too disconnected from all it stood for.

Fast forward to Summer 2001; James had turned fifteen and was working at a local restaurant. 'A guy wearing a Perranporth Mission hoodie came in. We got talking, and I discovered that he was the Mission's leader! He invited me to come to the beach mission the following year. Previously, I'd only been to the beach mission because Mum took me, not because I was invited, but now, with a personal invite, I resolved to return. I still remembered the kindness of the team, and that something about them was different.'

I once was lost and now am found

'The next summer, I went to the Mission, I asked loads of questions. But the real breakthrough came when a couple shared one evening how they had faced a really difficult situation and God had answered their prayers in a wonderful way.

'Afterwards, everyone went back to playing games and having fun, but I found myself unable to move from the table where I sat. I began to weep uncontrollably – I hid by flipping my hoodie over my head. I had been trying to carry so many things for so long, and suddenly I realised that despite the mistakes and wrong decisions I'd made, God forgave me. I accepted his forgiveness and felt his presence. His love entered into my heart, and he lifted all those burdens off my shoulders.

'As I wept, the Mission leaders would sit next to me and put their arm around me and show me that they were there for me. And as I peered up at other people through my teary eyes, I felt an overwhelming sense of love for them – a love so strong that if someone had asked, I would have died for them. And that's what set that experience apart from any other religion or faith, philosophy or idea, because I believe what I experienced was that sacrificial love for others that Jesus holds in his heart.

'That was my "born again" moment when I repented. I came out of the church feeling free and light. The Holy Spirit was working powerfully in my heart, and it was the start of the healing process for me. And from that time, having always struggled with reading, I was suddenly able to read my Bible, understand it, apply it, and it gave me life. That to me was nothing short of miraculous.'

Grace my fears relieved...

The next summer James was on the Mission team. One evening, he had another incredible encounter with the Holy Spirit. 'I was hit by this amazing feeling of knowing I was totally accepted by God, just as I was. I felt whole and complete, filled with joy, utterly at peace and at one with myself. The body dysmorphia was gone, and I no longer felt self-conscious or any need to prove myself or compare myself to other people. I didn't know how to explain what was happening to me. It's like I got a glimpse of eternity.'

As John Newton expressed his faith experiences in song, James started expressing his in rap and poetry:

I am a lion tamed by the Lamb,
holy and healing in God's hands, I am.
Safe on your wings, carry me you can.

Unfold your plan for the world to see,
let healing be. Put me on my knees,
the dark deceives, the animal in me
breathes.

Let us all know new realities,
open the door, I want to be free like a
bird that soars,
in you, I believe I'm a lion that roars.

From once touched now wanting more.
Hand of the Lamb, heal this hurting land.
Let your love pour and let your stream of
life explore.

The Lord has promised good to me

A few years on, Perranporth Mission's leader invited James to do a church internship in the Midlands. Later, another friend from Perranporth Mission exhorted him to do an internship with DNA, a national organisation which equips people for church leadership. She helped to fund his placement, which was at her church in Essex.

From there, James spent two years on the house team and pastoral team at Lee Abbey, before completing a degree in theology at Trinity College in Bristol. More recently, he spent three years as a Methodist lay pastor in Cornwall, and in September 2021 he took up a post as minister of North Street Church in Taunton, his wife's home town.

'I'm loving being part of the church family here and leading it as we go forward. We have a congregation of about twenty on a Sunday morning, but we've just partnered with a local contemporary worship group and we've launched an evening gathering, focused on prayer and worship. Around fifty people are coming, some from other churches and some with no church connections at all. In the last few weeks several people have asked if they could be baptised.

'God has done fantastic things in my life. He's met all my needs. He's put me in a position where I'm able to feel fulfilled, and he's entrusted me with a huge responsibility of pastoring God's people. I can't really describe the level of gratitude I feel towards him. And I'm also so thankful to SU, the Perranporth Mission and those involved, because collectively they played a huge part in my discovering God's amazing grace for myself.'

At Scripture Union, we're passionate about seeing non-church children and young people like James discover a personal, vibrant faith in Jesus. To find out more about our work, and to provide your support through your gifts and prayers or through volunteering at events like Perranporth, visit scriptureunion.org.uk. For more stories like this, subscribe to Connecting You, our free quarterly supporter magazine, at su.org.uk/connectingyou

Earthly stories, heavenly meanings

Many years ago, as a schools' worker with Scripture Union, I used to feel nervous and on edge if another staff member turned up at an assembly I was taking, or at a camp I was leading. My reaction was unfounded. They were there to support me – and I always ended up feeling encouraged!

Jesus, however, was under constant scrutiny by angry and resentful religious teachers who, rather than supporting and encouraging him as he taught about God, hated him and wanted to trap him. He was aware that they were looking for an excuse to arrest and kill him. How hard that hostility must have been. After all, he was human!

Jesus dealt with them so perceptively, sometimes with a question and often with a parable about salvation and living God's way. However, these parables added fuel to the fire. The scholarly Pharisees would have been aware which characters in each story referred to them – the meaning was obvious. Often, they had nothing to say in response, and Jesus managed to leave them totally wrong-footed. His shrewd, authoritative answers to their questions embarrassed them and exposed their evil motives. As a result, they became even more determined to kill him.

It was about the timing. God's timing. Eventually they would succeed in their wicked plan, but, as always, God would have the last word. 'But thanks be to God! He gives us the victory through our Lord Jesus Christ' (1 Corinthians 15:57). And, despite everything that Jesus had to cope with, what shone through? God's amazing grace!

About the writer
Sue Clutterham

A former Local Mission Partner with Scripture Union, Sue enjoys writing and editing material that helps people of all ages to explore the Bible in creative ways. Free time includes walking, reading and watching crime thrillers, as well as outings with friends and family to local tea shops. Her favourite place in the world is a deserted beach.

Sunday 1 January

Psalm 77

Happy New Year!

PREPARE

As we look ahead at the beginning of a new year, take some time to recall God's 'amazing grace', now and throughout history.

READ

Psalm 77

EXPLORE

The words of this song are timely! Perhaps, like the psalmist in verses 7 to 9, you've had moments of doubting God, especially over the last few years, as we succumbed to a global pandemic. And yet, as we revisit the past, we see God's faithfulness time and time again, throughout history and in our own lives too: his miracles, his works and his mighty deeds (vs 11,12). A reminder that God's ways are holy and perfect, displaying his power to rescue us.

The reference to the parting of the Red Sea (v 19) is a reminder of the people of Israel, hotly pursued by the Egyptians they were escaping from, confronted by water and seemingly trapped. As they reached an apparent dead end after all that they had already been through, I can't help wondering if they might have thought, '*Now* what?'

'The God who performs miracles' (v 14) provided a way through the sea! What a great illustration of God's promise in Isaiah 43:2: 'When you pass through the waters, I will be with you; and when you pass through the rivers, they will not sweep over you.' Whatever confronts us, God himself is with us!

Your ways, God, are holy. What god is as great as our God?

Psalm 77:13

RESPOND

Remember God's faithfulness. Thank him for his amazing grace. Praise him for his mighty deeds. Ask him to help you trust him, whatever he has in store for you.

Bible in a year: Genesis 1,2; Matthew 1

Monday 2 January
Luke 14:1–14

Judge not…

PREPARE

Most of us know people whom we don't find easy and struggle with, although they may be blissfully unaware of it! What is our response to them? How *should* we respond?

READ

Luke 14:1–14

EXPLORE

At least one step ahead of his critics, Jesus is gracious. Aware of their motives, he responds to the hostility of the Pharisees with carefully constructed questions about the importance of showing mercy. The result? Jesus turns the tables on their scheming yet again. They have nothing to say (vs 4,6).

But Jesus is not afraid to confront hypocrisy and – although the Bible does not tell us how the guests responded to his comments – there are lessons to be learned from his candid observation of their desire for prestige (vs 7–11). Service is much more important than status. Humility, in itself, is a sign of greatness.

In verses 12–14, Jesus refers to the marginalised people overlooked by society. His comments about treating everyone with kindness are directed to his host, but are equally pertinent for us today. They are similar to the words from the book of Isaiah, which Jesus proclaims in the synagogue at Nazareth at the start of his ministry. Then, they were well received (Luke 4:20–22), but now the tide is beginning to turn against him…

> 'For all those who exalt themselves will be humbled, and those who humble themselves will be exalted.'
>
> **Luke 14:11**

RESPOND

Are you guilty of seeking status, or judging others, in what you think or say? Read Philippians 2:3–7. Pray for a humble attitude and a kind, servant heart. Thank God for Jesus' supreme example of humility and service.

Bible in a year: Genesis 3,4; Matthew 2

Tuesday 3 January

Luke 14:15–24

Excuses, excuses

PREPARE

Do you have neighbours, friends or relatives who are indifferent to the good news of Jesus? Pray for them now. Ask God to give them a sense of need, so that they hear his invitation and respond (Isaiah 55:1,5).

READ

Luke 14:15–24

EXPLORE

I'm ashamed to admit that I once booked an appointment at a specific time in order to avoid accepting an unwanted invitation. I guess that it was not unlike the characters in this punchy parable. This story is Jesus' response to one of the guests, whose comment (v 15) probably means that he thought only Jews would be present in God's kingdom. Jesus subsequently turns that notion upside down!

The master in the story is God, the great banquet is the kingdom, and the invited guests represent the Jewish nation who would reject Jesus (John 1:11). The feeble excuses for declining the invitation show total disinterest in what is on offer – for example, buying land or livestock would surely involve preliminary inspection! All the reasons given show other priorities taking precedence – something we may also need to be mindful of, perhaps?

Jesus' response towards those who reject his offer of salvation is to emphasise yet again that he came to save not only the Jews, but Gentiles too. It includes the marginalised (people the Pharisees would have considered 'unclean', vs 21,23). Jesus knows exactly what he is doing, and the hidden message is loud and clear for the Pharisees.

'Blessed is the one who will eat at the feast in the kingdom of God.'

Luke 14:15

RESPOND

Jesus' attitude to outcasts demonstrates the heart of God so clearly. Do we take God's grace and mercy for granted?

Bible in a year: Genesis 5,6; Matthew 3

It was never going to be easy!

PREPARE

What is the hardest thing for you at the moment in your walk with Jesus? Ask for his strength and perseverance to keep going.

READ

Luke 14:25–35

EXPLORE

Seemingly harsh words from Jesus. Is he *really* asking us to hate others, especially our loved ones? Jesus is using hyperbolic language here. Just as in Matthew 18:8,9 he refers to gouging out eyes and cutting off hands, he is making extravagant statements, not intended to be taken literally but used to emphasise the importance of what he is teaching. Our primary allegiance must be to Jesus, rather than family.

The reference to carrying our cross reminds us that it cost Jesus everything to do God's will, so it won't be easy for us. The illustrations Jesus uses of counting the cost (literally) in verses 28–30 and being in charge of an army going to war (vs 31–33) speak for themselves. The final reference to salt (v 34) is a reminder of our need to make a significant difference to others and the world we live in by the way we live – a tough challenge in itself.

'Salvation in Jesus is not merely a transaction. It is, at heart, a covenantal relationship. And no relationship lasts without loyal commitments and actions... Jesus' command to "Follow me" is both gift and demand.'*

'And whoever does not carry their cross and follow me cannot be my disciple.'

Luke 14:27

RESPOND

Following Jesus is all or nothing. Use the opportunity of this new year, with the fresh start that it brings, to re-commit yourself to high cost, whole-hearted discipleship.

*Jeannine K Brown, www.workingpreacher.org/commentaries/revised-common-lectionary/ordinary-23-3/commentary-on-luke-1425-33

Bible in a year: Genesis 7,8; Psalms 1,2

Thursday 5 January

Luke 15:1–10

The Lord is my shepherd

PREPARE

As we think about this well-known parable, focus on anyone you know who is like the lost sheep in the story because they have wandered away from God. Ask Jesus to rescue them.

READ

Luke 15:1–10

EXPLORE

Modern shepherding involves sheepdogs, mobile phones and quad bikes. It's hard work, but very different from biblical times, when shepherds often had a relationship with their flock.

Jesus tells this story in response to the Pharisees' ongoing hostility (vs 1,2). They have just complained that Jesus is associating with sinners so, once again, he lets them have it! His listeners are all too familiar with the scenario of a runaway sheep. However, shepherds in those days – many of whom were not renowned for their integrity – might weigh up the cost and leave a lost creature to its fate, so there is a twist...

This parable should be called 'The good shepherd' (vs 3–7). Later, Jesus would describe himself in this way, his ministry to his 'flock' culminating in the ultimate sacrifice (John 10:11–18). The message is clear. God actively seeks those who are 'lost' and rejoices when they are 'found'. When the lost are rescued, it leads to restoration and new life in his presence. The second parable of the lost coin reminds us just how precious we are to God (Deuteronomy 14:2).

'In the same way, I tell you, there is rejoicing in the presence of the angels of God over one sinner who repents.'

Luke 15:10

RESPOND

We may have been rescued by God, but following his way, rather than ours, is a daily process. Each time – like sheep – we turn away from our loving Shepherd, he searches for us and rescues us. Thank him now.

Bible in a year: Genesis 9–11; Matthew 4

Friday 6 January
Luke 15:11–32

A very familiar story

PREPARE

Ask God to give you fresh insight as you read this well-known, hugely significant parable.

READ

Luke 15:11–32

EXPLORE

Another story about being lost and found! But it's a person rather than an animal or precious object who is lost – and rather than active seeking, this time there is patient waiting. There should be a different name for this well-known parable too – the magnitude of God's amazing patience and grace might be better described with the title 'The loving father'.

Whatever causes the rift in the family, the son chooses to go his own way, with disastrous consequences, but a very happy ending (despite a jealous and petulant sibling). Familiar scenario? Of course! They may not be so dramatic, but similar events are played out in people's lives on a regular basis.

This is about us. This is about our daily walk with God. This reminds us of the many times we are selfish and greedy and turn our backs on God. When his son finally returns home, does the father say, 'How many times have I told you not to...?' He has watched and waited patiently for his errant boy to come to his senses. He offers no recrimination. He welcomes him back extravagantly, restoring him to his position of beloved son with unqualified forgiveness and undeserved grace. It speaks for itself.

'... this brother of yours was dead and is alive again; he was lost and is found.'

Luke 15:32

RESPOND

Use these words from Psalm 79:8,9 to pray to your loving Father:
'... may your mercy come quickly to meet us, for we are in desperate need. Help us, God our Saviour ... and forgive our sins.'

Bible in a year: Genesis 12,13; Matthew 5

Saturday 7 January

Luke 16:1–18

A heavenly perspective

PREPARE

In our society driven by desire for wealth and prestige, this lesser-known parable of Jesus gives us a down-to-earth and interesting angle on being *in* the world, but not *of* the world (see 1 John 2:16). Who are *we* 'serving' (v 13)?

READ

Luke 16:1–18

EXPLORE

Jesus directs this teaching to his disciples (v 1). However, he also has a subtle message for the hostile Pharisees (vs 14,15). The political tension is building, and they are looking for an opportunity to arrest him. So far, Jesus has skilfully avoided each trap as it is set. The time is not yet right for God's plan of salvation to be fulfilled.

The parable itself is in verses 1–8, with the application from verses 9–18. In this unusual story, Jesus commends foresight and prudence and encourages us to be shrewd in our dealings with others, without being dishonest ourselves. The key to this is in verse 13. Our focus needs to be on following Jesus, so that we can deal with worldly distractions with integrity. Not surprisingly, the Pharisees' response in verse 14 brings a hard-hitting rebuke from Jesus (v 15). However, this also challenges us to examine our attitudes, motives and lifestyle honestly. Are all the resources we have at our disposal available for God to use, as he wishes?

'God knows your hearts.'

Luke 16:15

RESPOND

God's words to Samuel in 1 Samuel 16:7 are a salutary reminder to be beyond reproach in the way we live. Ask God to strengthen you as you follow him. Thank him for his forgiveness for times that you fail.

Bible in a year: Genesis 14,15; Psalms 3,4

Sunday 8 January

Psalm 78

Lessons from his story

PREPARE

Over the past week, which of the parables has challenged you most? Ask God to help you apply its teaching to your life.

READ

Psalm 78

EXPLORE

This psalm is very relevant to our readings over the past seven days. In verses 1–3, David's prophetic words remind us how important it is to take note of Jesus' teaching and put it into practice.

'We will tell the next generation the praiseworthy deeds of the LORD' (v 4) is a hugely significant verse for Scripture Union, whose primary mission is to reach the majority of children and young people who are not in church (95 per cent of children and young people in England and Wales, for example). We aim to create opportunities for 'the 95' to explore the Bible, respond to Jesus and grow in faith. We long to see a new generation who have a vibrant and personal Christian faith, because they have met with God through his Word.

As we read through this psalm, with its reminders of God's dealings with his people in the Old Testament, our prayer is that contacts we make and relationships we build with neighbours, friends and colleagues will have the outcome of verse 7, '... they would put their trust in God'.

Along with Jesus' parables, these verses are testimony to God's unfailing love, his faithfulness, his patience, his forgiveness and his grace. Praise him!

... listen to the words of my mouth. I will open my mouth with a parable.

Psalm 78:1,2

RESPOND

Read verse 4 again. Pray for Scripture Union staff, associates and volunteers as they reach out with the gospel to children and young people who have no knowledge of him.

Bible in a year: Genesis 16,17; Matthew 6

Monday 9 January

Luke 16:19–31

Rich and poor

PREPARE

What is your attitude towards the rich, and also to those who are poor?

READ

Luke 16:19–31

EXPLORE

These sobering words from Jesus challenge us now, as well as his listeners at the time. The Pharisees consider wealth desirable (Luke 16:14), so are wrong-footed by a story about a poor man being rewarded and a rich man punished. In this parable of contrasts, Jesus is not teaching that it is wrong to be wealthy or that poverty is a virtue. He is warning that our destiny is determined in this life not by what we do, or accumulate, but by our response to God.

First we see both men in this life and then in the life to come. The rich man (sometimes referred to as 'Dives', which is Latin for 'rich') uses his money selfishly, with no regard at all for the obvious need of the diseased beggar at his gate. Lazarus – whose name means 'God has helped' – is welcomed into God's presence. Meanwhile, the rich man ends up in torment and separated from God (vs 23,24).

How ironic are Jesus' words in verse 31! They are the response to the rich man's desperate request that Lazarus be sent to warn his family of the perils of rejecting God. Even the subsequent resurrection of the Son of God himself would fail to convince many (then and now) of the need to turn to him.

> 'If they do not listen to Moses and the Prophets, they will not be convinced even if someone rises from the dead.'
>
> **Luke 16:31**

RESPOND

Pray for people you know who have not yet turned to God. Ask God to help you share the good news of Jesus, so that they may respond to him.

Bible in a year: Genesis 18,19; Matthew 7

Luke 17:1 – 19:27

On the road with Jesus

About the writer
Peter Stone

Peter lives in Sydney, Australia and is part of the team of SU NSW. He's a graduate of Regent College in Vancouver. He works as a consultant in business strategy and leadership development.

Are you a fan of 'road trip' movies? If you are, you'll particularly enjoy our time in Luke's Gospel. We're dropping in on Jesus and his disciples as they journey towards Jerusalem. Like all road trips, we don't always know what is around the corner ahead. We will see Jesus do some amazing things. We will eavesdrop on some conversations. We will be surprised as Jesus says some quite outrageous things.

I promise that you will find some of the narrative challenging and even confronting. Sometimes we will feel the cultural gap between the twenty-first and first centuries as quite wide. Sometimes we will wonder what Jesus really meant or was really thinking. No matter. As Luke says right at the opening of his Gospel, he is seeking to give an 'orderly account' (Luke 1:3). Luke has already laid a foundation in chapters 1 to 16, where we see Jesus as powerful, courageous, compassionate, purposeful and sent: the Son of God who has come to seek and save the lost.

Luke's mission continues: 'that you may know the certainty of the things you have been taught' (Luke 1:4). We do this in the context of a volatile world where there is pain and injustice alongside hope and joy. Certainty is in short supply. Like the disciples, we can only know peace when we follow the Prince of Peace. Enjoy the journey on the road with Jesus.

Tuesday 10 January

Luke 17:1–10

So watch yourselves!

PREPARE

Would you describe yourself more as a realist or an idealist? Which approach to life do you aspire to? Today, Jesus will speak into both those realities.

READ

Luke 17:1–10

EXPLORE

Stand in the shoes of the disciples for a moment. Jesus launches a missile in verse 2, then another in verse 6, then yet another in verse 10. All hit their target: how our faith affects our daily lives. He calls them to square up to the reality of a fallen world, but then calls them to live as though that world is fully in God's control.

Their response in verse 5 is both achingly simple and deeply profound. Faced with the challenge of living as God's faithful servants, their first awareness is of their own inadequacy. That's the right place to start! There are no heroic Christians, only faithful ones through whom God does heroic things.

Discipleship demands that we address the reality of temptation and sin in our lives and the lives of those around us. Bad stuff *will* happen. But (and it's a big but) the real issue for us is how we respond: ridiculous levels of genuine forgiveness, outrageous faith in God's power to intervene, servant-heartedness as we go about living for him. And underneath all is the determination *not* to be the cause of sin in the lives of others.

The apostles said to the Lord, 'Increase our faith!'

Luke 17:5

RESPOND

Who do you need to forgive? What mountain have you given up trying to move? What sin are you failing to confront? Where have you fallen into the trap of thinking that God owes you something?

Bible in a year: Genesis 20,21; Matthew 8

Wednesday 11 January
Luke 17:11–19

Faith-filled thankfulness

PREPARE

Reflect on the difference between genuine thanks and merely being polite. 'Thank you' can mean almost nothing – or it might change the direction of our whole life...

READ

Luke 17:11–19

EXPLORE

In a world where even machines say 'thank you' in response to our actions, it is easy to lose our grip on the power of those two words. Genuine thankfulness is our acknowledgement that something was done by another person who had the choice to ignore or discount our needs in favour of their own comfort or preference. (See 2 Corinthians 8:9.)

Jesus is on his way to Jerusalem. He knows what awaits him there. He is focused. Yet he stops to listen and respond to the most disposable people imaginable: lepers on the Samaritan border. Twice.

The first time ten people are yelling. That would be hard to ignore, even at a distance. They have a need Jesus can and does meet. The second time only one person is yelling, but because of a very different need. The healed Samaritan is no longer at a distance (verse 16). He is driven by joy, not pain. He is drawn close to the source of his joy. He cannot be silent or self-focused.

His thanks do not change Jesus, but they certainly change him. His whole world has been reoriented with a new compass. The nine others were healed. He has been 'made well' (v 19).

> He threw himself at Jesus' feet and thanked him – and he was a Samaritan.
>
> **Luke 17:16**

RESPOND

'Rise and go.' What would it mean for you to obey this command today? Who would be blessed as a result?

Bible in a year: Genesis 22,23; Psalms 5,6

Thursday 12 January
Luke 17:20–37

Signs of the times

PREPARE

John Lennon famously said, 'Life is what happens when you're busy making other plans.' When has that been true in your experience? In your experience of God?

READ

Luke 17:20–37

EXPLORE

Luke suddenly changes perspective from the personal to the cosmic. He zooms out to a wide shot. It is not a pretty picture (see v 37)!

The passage opens with a question about 'when' (v 20) but ends with one about 'where' (v 37). It is important to ask the right question! Jesus completely reframes the Pharisees' issue from an obsession with signs (which is really about being clever), to the vital concern of response (which is really about obedience). Signs are external. Response is on the inside (v 21).

Church history is littered with groups confidently predicting Jesus' return in response to interpreting 'signs'. They all look foolish. Jesus could not have made it clearer (see Mark 13:32). That is none of our business. What counts is whether we are ready for the day, every day. How we live is of much greater importance than how cleverly we think we can predict Jesus' return.

The kingdom of God is within (among) us. That reality should inform every relationship, our life priorities and our perspective in the midst of challenges.

> 'For the Son of Man in his day will be like the lightning, which flashes and lights up the sky from one end to the other.'
>
> **Luke 17:24**

RESPOND

Perhaps today is the one Jesus is referring to in verse 24. In that moment everything else becomes redundant. How should that possibility affect how you live for him today?

Bible in a year: Genesis 24,25; Matthew 9

Friday 13 January
Luke 18:1–8

Always pray. Never give up

PREPARE

Why do you pray? How do you think God feels about your prayers? Be honest. He can cope!

READ

Luke 18:1–8

EXPLORE

Unlike with some parables, here we are told bluntly what this one is all about (v 1). What is unusual in this story is that it teaches us what our Father is *not* like. He is *not* distant, uncaring, grumpy, self-focused or merely pragmatic (vs 4,5). He is close. He is loving. He listens. And above all, he is powerful and eager to act (vs 7,8).

This leaves us with an interesting challenge. Why should we persist in prayer and why doesn't God usually drop everything and answer our prayers as we would like? For many of us it often feels like we're dealing with the judge in the parable. It's as though we need to get his attention by our persistence and wear him down until he gives in and answers us.

Prayer is part of a bigger scheme. When we pray, we are not letting God know about something that has skipped his attention. Nor are we letting him in on news he hasn't heard yet. Prayer doesn't change God. Prayer changes us! It is God's way of letting us into his mind and heart so that we might be changed into his likeness and join in his agenda for his world.

'I tell you, he will see that they get justice, and quickly.'

Luke 18:8a

RESPOND

Reflect on Romans 8:26,27: '... the Spirit intercedes for God's people in accordance with the will of God.' Quieten your heart and mind. What is God moving you to pray about today?

Bible in a year: Genesis 26,27; Matthew 10

Saturday 14 January

Luke 18:9–17

The upside-down kingdom

PREPARE

Who is the last person in the world you would expect to walk into your church and ask for prayer? How would you respond if they turned up this Sunday?

READ

Luke 18:9–17

EXPLORE

Again, Luke leaves no doubt about what Jesus was saying. Many non-Christians in Western societies would see verse 9 as an accurate caricature of many churchgoers! So, we should listen carefully.

The Pharisee approaches a God who owes him something and he wants everyone to hear about that (vs 11,12). The tax collector hides his face as he seeks forgiveness from a God who knows his weakness. The contrast could not be greater. Next it is the disciples who get it all wrong (v 15) when they tell off people who dare to annoy Jesus with their smelly, noisy children. They know that he has bigger fish to fry.

Jesus is blunt in both instances. It is the tax collector who is justified and the children who are the exemplars. He turns everything on its head, and then gives it a good shake. Mark 10:13–16 tells the same story, but adds the final detail that Jesus picked up the children, held them and blessed them. This kingdom is like no other. This king is like no other. The last shall be first, the weak made strong, the poor become rich.

> 'Truly I tell you, anyone who will not receive the kingdom of God like a little child will never enter it.'
>
> **Luke 18:17**

RESPOND

You have nowhere to hide and nothing to bring. And yet God loves you beyond measure. Thank him afresh that there is a place ready for you in the Father's house (John 14:2).

Bible in a year: Genesis 28,29; Psalms 7,8

Sunday 15 January
Psalm 78:40–72

Dummies' guide to grieving God

PREPARE

What pattern of sin keeps repeating in your life? What would it take to disrupt it? Bring that to God now. He's always ready to forgive and forget.

READ

Psalm 78:40–72

EXPLORE

Over and again the writers of the Old Testament take us back to the wonders of the Exodus of the Israelites from Egypt and their subsequent 40 years in the wilderness (vs 52–55). Somehow this generation managed to both walk through the sea on dry land and then despair of God's seeming powerlessness to meet their most basic needs (vs 40–42,56). They react in the moment, seeming incapable of trusting God for the long haul. Just like you and me!

This psalm is a chronicle of failures and new beginnings, of sin and forgiveness, of despair and hope. It revisits the Exodus debacle, but positions it in the context of God's overarching plan. In the midst of all the mess, God is at work. A young shepherd will inherit a promise about a kingdom that is without end (vs 70–72). Despite all their failings, the people of God will know a king who has 'integrity of heart'. David had moments where this characteristic was evident. But more importantly he had a Son who will sit on his throne for ever (Isaiah 9:6,7).

Again and again they put God to the test; they vexed the Holy One of Israel.

Psalm 78:41

RESPOND

Like Paul we may feel 'wretched' about our capacity to sin (Romans 7:24), but read Romans 8:1–4. The pattern of Psalm 78 is broken by God through Jesus. There is no place for guilt and despair. God's anger has been dealt with. Praise him.

Bible in a year: Genesis 30,31; Matthew 11

Monday 16 January

Luke 18:18–30

Come, follow me

PREPARE

What do you truly value above everything else? That is the big question Jesus will ask you today. Get ready to answer him.

READ

Luke 18:18–30

EXPLORE

This passage has nothing to do with wealth and everything to do with priorities. It appears also in Mark 10:17–30 and Matthew 19:16–29. Like most Jewish people at that time, Jesus' disciples saw wealth as a sign of God's blessing and approval (v 26). If this man doesn't make the grade, then the rest of us should simply give up trying. Or so it seems.

Jesus has already made the point clearly in Luke 12:34: 'Where your treasure is, there your heart will be also.' John Calvin expresses this truth in his famous assessment that 'The human heart is a perpetual idol factory.'* We have a problem of eternal consequence that we simply cannot solve on our own. Left to our own devices we will make it worse day by day.

The only hope is if God intervenes and actually changes us from the inside out. Jesus assures us that this miracle is already under way in verse 27. But wait (as they say in the TV advertisements): there's more! Not only can we be saved, but also richly blessed (vs 29,30). Our eternal future is not in some grey refugee camp but in abundant life with a loving Father.

Jesus replied, 'What is impossible with man is possible with God.'

Luke 18:27

RESPOND

Jesus' command to the ruler applies to us today: put everything aside and follow him. There is no other way. Take a moment to reflect on Hebrews 12:1.

*John Calvin, *Institutes of the Christian Religion*, 1536

Bible in a year: Genesis 32,33; Matthew 12

Tuesday 17 January
Luke 18:31–43

Open my eyes

PREPARE

What harsh reality is troubling you? What aspect of your life would you like God to change?

READ

Luke 18:31–43

EXPLORE

There are two forms of blindness on display in this passage. The first involves the disciples as they completely fail to process Jesus' concise summary of what awaits him – and them – when they get to Jerusalem (vs 31–33). They are unaware of their blindness. The second is about a man whose physical eyesight has failed (v 35). He is acutely aware of his blindness. Both will require a miracle if healing is to occur.

On several occasions Jesus told his disciples plainly and bluntly that he would be rejected, tried and murdered in Jerusalem (see Mark 8:31–33 and 9:30–32; Matthew 16:21–28; Luke 9:22–27). At each instance they completely miss the point, or even challenge Jesus to change the narrative. This is in such contrast to the immediate response of the blind man. He joyfully praises God and follows Jesus (v 43).

The issue of wilful blindness crops up many times in the Gospels. It is usually a refusal to confront reality because it is some combination of scary, embarrassing or inconvenient. It is only when we can see the truth of who Jesus is, what he has done and what that all means that we are able to navigate the world with our eyes wide open.

'Lord, I want to see.'

Luke 18:41b

RESPOND

Is there anything God wants to show you that you're reluctant to engage with? He loves to open the eyes of the blind. Ask for that miracle today.

Bible in a year: Genesis 34–36; Matthew 13

Wednesday 18 January

Luke 19:1–10

Look who's coming to dinner

PREPARE

Where did Jesus first find you? Were you seeking him? Or did he take the initiative?

READ

Luke 19:1–10

EXPLORE

Today we encounter another outsider who desperately wants to see. Zacchaeus would have looked so foolish and 'out there' as he climbed that tree (v 4). Like the rich ruler of Luke 18:18, he actively seeks to engage with Jesus, but like the tax collector of Luke 18:13, he decides to keep his distance. It is Jesus who takes hold of Zacchaeus, a short, morally compromised outsider, with the words, 'I must stay at your house today' (v 5).

The rich ruler walks away despondent because he realises that his possessions were more important than he thought. Zacchaeus spontaneously realises that his possessions are getting in the way of what he really wants, so he lets them go (v 8). The ruler had high social standing. Zacchaeus was held in contempt (v 7). The ruler refuses Jesus' invitation. Zacchaeus is overjoyed by the privilege (v 6). The contrast between these two could not be greater.

Luke has been weaving the fabric of his message for several chapters. In this upside-down kingdom, the blind see, the rich turn away and the sons of Abraham include the least likely because of the deep, loving truth of verse 10. This king is like no other.

> Jesus ... looked up and said to him, 'Zacchaeus, come down immediately. I must stay at your house today.'
>
> **Luke 19:5**

RESPOND

Reflect on Revelation 3:20 afresh. Jesus longs for fellowship with you. What would it mean for you to welcome him as gladly as Zacchaeus did?

Bible in a year: Genesis 37,38; Psalm 9

Surprise ending

PREPARE

What talents and resources has God entrusted to you? What fruit is there to show?

READ

Luke 19:11–27

EXPLORE

Read verse 11 again. Jesus is still at Zacchaeus' home and is talking about who is (and isn't) part of his kingdom. There is a crowd around him talking excitedly about their ideas of what this kingdom will mean for them. Jesus uses this most confronting story to counter their expectations.

Again, Luke zooms out from the personal to the cosmic. The story of the 'minas' is really about how Israel has failed to fulfil God's purposes. Some *are* applauded for serving faithfully in small matters (v 17), but through their history, Israel have *not* been good stewards. Instead of glorifying God by obeying him and showing how to love and worship him, they have rejected him (v 14). They have been focused on status and tiny details, looking down on outsiders (like Zacchaeus?) rather than welcoming them in. God's people have rejected the prophets and their message of repentance (vs 20–23). They have not borne the fruit that was expected. This will have serious consequences (v 27).

Jesus wants the crowd to know that God will fulfil his own purposes and the outcome will not be what Israel generally expects. The next step in the journey will be Jesus' entry into Jerusalem where this contrast will be stark.

> His divine power has given us everything we need for a godly life through our knowledge of him who called us by his own glory and goodness.
>
> **2 Peter 1:3**

RESPOND

'Nothing in my hand I bring, simply to thy cross I cling ... helpless look to thee for grace' ('Rock of ages', Augustus Toplady). Thank God for what Jesus has done for you.

Bible in a year: Genesis 39,40; Matthew 14

Scripture Union
By purchasing *Daily Bread*, you are helping to support Scripture Union's mission with children and young people. Thank you!
Subscribe to our free supporter and prayer magazine at su.org.uk/connectingyou

Enjoying God's welcome

Leviticus can feel like hard work! Maybe it's because after the fast-moving storylines of Genesis and Exodus, the rules and regulations of Leviticus seem a bit... well... boring. Or maybe, it's because the rituals and laws seem so archaic and irrelevant. So, what is going on in the 27 chapters that make up this book?

Well, to state the obvious, Leviticus follows right after Exodus. In Exodus, God's people – recently rescued from Egypt – have to learn how to live as God's 'treasured possession' (Exodus 19:5,6). The second half of the book of Exodus describes the special holy place that Moses was to build, so that God himself may 'dwell among them' (Exodus 25:8). Exodus closes as God himself moved in among his people (Exodus 40:34). For the first time since Eden, God lived right in the centre of his people: the great rift (Genesis 3:24) had been healed!

Now the challenge is how to maintain that intimate relationship and not to lose it again. Leviticus addresses that concern: how to safely enjoy God's welcome. Through rituals and festivals (chapters 1–7; 23–27); through the work of a priesthood (chapters 8–10; 21,22); through rules defining what is clean and unclean (chapters 11–15; 17–20), and above all through the central Day of Atonement celebration (chapter 16), God spells out how Israel can enjoy his presence and be the distinct people of a holy God (11:44,45).

Hard work it may be – but well worth the effort!

About the writer
David Lawrence

David is currently the Teaching Pastor at Thornbury Baptist Church, near Bristol. In the past, he has worked with Scripture Union, ForMission (Springdale College), the Methodist Church of Great Britain and the London Institute for Contemporary Christianity.

Friday 20 January

Leviticus 1:1–17

The call to friendship

PREPARE

'I have been crucified with Christ and I no longer live, but Christ lives in me' (Galatians 2:20a). What encourages you most: that you are dead to self, or that you are alive in Christ? Turn your thoughts into prayer.

READ

Leviticus 1:1–17

EXPLORE

The all-powerful Creator God calls out to his people and invites them to approach him (vs 1,2) – awesome! The appropriate form of approach is *sacrifice*, and rules are given for what is acceptable and how to perform the rituals. The cost is high: only the best will do (1:3,10; see also 2:1,4). Only *perfect* sacrifices count when approaching a holy God!

The offer of blood (vs 5,11,15) may puzzle and even repel us, but its significance is found in Leviticus 17:11. The blood is the *life* of the animal, offered on behalf of the worshipper. The wholehearted yielding of one's whole life to God is the very essence of biblical sacrifice.

But if only *perfect, totally yielded* people can approach God, then what hope for us?

As Christians, our approach to God is made possible by the final and ultimate sacrifice – that of Jesus, who 'loved us and offered *himself* as a sacrifice for us' and in him we too become 'a pleasing aroma to God' (1:9,13,17; Ephesians 5:2, NLT).

> 'Speak to the Israelites and say to them: "When anyone among you brings an offering to the LORD, bring as your offering an animal from either the herd or the flock".'
>
> **Leviticus 1:2**

RESPOND

'The life I now live in the body, I live by faith in the Son of God, who loved me and gave himself for me' (Galatians 2:20b). Think of your day's schedule and ask for faith for the 'life you now live'.

Bible in a year: Genesis 41,42; Matthew 15

Saturday 21 January
Leviticus 3:1–17

Lord, you have my kidneys!

PREPARE

Quieten yourself and use these words as a prayer to centre yourself in God's love and acceptance: 'Jesus has brought me to his house and God is rejoicing over my arrival' (see Luke 15:6).

READ

Leviticus 3:1–17

EXPLORE

After the sin (atonement, 1:4) and cereal offerings (2:1), we now read about the 'fellowship' or 'peace' offering. There are similarities with the other sacrifices of chapters 1 and 2, but also several differences. Leviticus 7:11 tells us, for example, that these offerings were optional, not mandatory.

Do you wonder why the entrails and kidneys were singled out as an offering to God (vs 3,4,9,10,14,15)? In the Old Testament 'the fat' is a way of saying 'the best' (eg Genesis 45:18). The thought is: single out your best and yield it to God. The kidneys were viewed as the seat of a person's emotions and the place where their deepest thoughts were hidden (much like we think today of the heart). Offering the offal was saying to God: 'Have all of me, the deepest part of me: the part that others do not see but which is open to you alone.'

Our best and our very lives (our 'fat and blood,' v 17) belong to God. They are not ours to use as we will, but must always be yielded to him.

> 'From what you offer you are to present this food offering to the LORD: the internal organs and all the fat that is connected to them, both kidneys with the fat on them…'
>
> **Leviticus 3:14,15**

RESPOND

What might be your 'best' possession, your 'best' relationship, your 'best' ability? Is your 'best' offered to God? Pray now and thank God for these. What might you do if you feel you are holding anything back?

Bible in a year: Genesis 43,44; Psalm 10

Sunday 22 January

Psalm 79

Praise after the pain

PREPARE

Think of one spiritual blessing, one material blessing and one relational blessing (from a friend, family or church perhaps) that you have received this week. Spend some time praising God for these and for all that he has provided.

READ

Psalm 79

EXPLORE

This psalm seems to have been written by eyewitnesses of the horrific scenes in Jerusalem when it was crushed by Nebuchadnezzar (589–587 BC). The callous violence of the first four verses speaks of horrific suffering, shame and loss. Almost worse than the physical suffering was the way in which God's name had been dragged through the mud by his people's collapse (vs 1–10).

The cry 'How long, LORD?' (v 5) resonates through the years, as Christian people try to marry the reality of persecution and suffering with their faith in a good and powerful, promise-keeping God. When pain and loss overwhelm us, there is only one place to go: to God for his mercy and deliverance (v 9).

The eyes of faith, though, see beyond the present to a different future. It makes all the difference – if we can – to endure suffering strengthened by *hope*. It is remarkable that a psalm that begins in such pain ends with the prospect of deliverance and praise (v 13).

> Then we your people, the sheep of your pasture, will praise you for ever; from generation to generation we will proclaim your praise.
>
> **Psalm 79:13**

RESPOND

'May the God of hope fill you with all joy and peace as you trust in him, so that you may overflow with hope by the power of the Holy Spirit' (Romans 15:13). Pray this verse over anyone you know who is facing hard times.

Bible in a year: Genesis 45,46; Matthew 16

Pollution alert

PREPARE

How is it with you and your heavenly Father right now? What words would you use to describe your relationship? Turn your thoughts into prayer.

READ

Leviticus 4:1 - 5:13

EXPLORE

It is a *long* reading! But in all these details of the sacrificial system it's important to remember what is going on. God was inviting his people to live with him, in close fellowship. The great obstacle to enjoying the blessings of that intimacy was sin: even *unintentional* sin polluted the worshipper and spoiled the relationship with a holy God (4:1,13,22,27; 5:2).

The good news here is that God is so keen to see things put to rights that he offers multiple ways for sacrifices to be made, by priests (4:3), the community as a whole (4:13), leaders (4:22) - in fact anyone at all (4:27), even the poorest in society (5:11). Instead of the worshipper bearing the penalty (5:6) for their sin, they were permitted to offer an animal in their place. The goal of 'atonement' (4:20,26,31,35; 5:6,10) - literally 'at-one-ment' - is secured by the price of the lifeblood of the sacrifice.

How wonderful to know that Jesus fulfils all these sacrifices, and his death covers even our unintentional sins (1 John 2:1,2).

'Say to the Israelites: "When anyone sins unintentionally and does what is forbidden in any of the LORD's commands..."'

Leviticus 4:2

RESPOND

'Oh, wonder of all wonders, that thro' thy death for me, my open sins, my secret sins, can all forgiven be ... Help me to take it in, what it meant to thee, the holy one, to bear away my sin' (Katherine Kelly, 1869–1942).

Bible in a year: Genesis 47,48; Matthew 17

Tuesday 24 January

Leviticus 5:14 – 6:7

Time to put things right

PREPARE

Have you had the experience of somebody that you had wronged forgiving you? How did that feel? What did it cost them?

READ

Leviticus 5:14 – 6:7

EXPLORE

In today's reading, we see our sin represented as a debt that we need to repay to God – and to anyone else that we may have short-changed or deceived (6:2,3).

Notice that the crime is against another person, but God takes it personally as unfaithfulness towards him (6:2). Any damage that we inflict at an interpersonal level grieves God. The psalmist, King David, understood that well. Following his adultery and murder of Uriah he prayed: 'Against you, you only, have I sinned and done what is evil in your sight' (Psalm 51:4). Since the sin offends both another person *and* God, the remedy is two-fold. A sacrificial animal pays for the guilt before God (5:15; 6:6), but the individual worshipper must also make amends for the damage they have done to others (5:16; 6:5).

It is in the spirit of this sacrifice that Jesus tells us that our encounter with God in worship must be accompanied by dealing with broken relationships: 'First go and be reconciled to [those you have hurt]; then come and offer your gift', is his instruction (Matthew 5:24).

'When they sin in any of these ways and realise their guilt, they must return what they have stolen ... or what was entrusted to them, or the lost property they found...'

Leviticus 6:4

RESPOND

Spend some moments allowing the Holy Spirit to bring to mind any situations where you may need to make amends. Pray about them and make a plan for how you intend to deal with them.

Bible in a year: Genesis 49,50; Matthew 18

Wednesday 25 January
Leviticus 6:24 – 7:38

Approach with awe

PREPARE

Try this, with the actions! 'O worship the Lord in the beauty of holiness; / Bow down before him, his glory proclaim; / With gold of obedience, and incense of lowliness, / Kneel and adore him: the Lord is his name' (JSB Monsell, 1811–75).

READ

Leviticus 6:24 – 7:38

EXPLORE

Did you just have a sense of déjà vu? Haven't we already read about these sacrifices before? Well spotted!

In chapters 1 to 5, the instructions for these same sacrifices were given to the Israelites (1:2): here now it is the priests that are in view (6:25). They needed to know how to handle the sacrifices that the individual Israelites brought. They also needed to know what share of which sacrifices they could legitimately keep for themselves (7:5,6,8,9,28–36).

All of these detailed instructions must have deepened the sense of awe in both the worshipper and the worship-leader (priests). They were handling holy things (6:25; 7:1) and breaking the rules had consequences (7:27). It was wonderful that God had made himself approachable, but how careful they had to be as they approached him!

'Approach with awe' should be the stance for New Testament worship too: 'Let us be thankful, and so worship God acceptably with reverence and awe, for our "God is a consuming fire"' (Hebrews 12:28,29).

' ... "These are the regulations for the sin offering: the sin offering is to be slaughtered before the LORD in the place where the burnt offering is slaughtered; it is most holy".'

Leviticus 6:25

RESPOND

How do we maintain the correct balance of *confidence* (Hebrews 4:16) and *reverence* as we enjoy God's welcome in gathered worship?

Bible in a year: Exodus 1,2; Psalms 11,12

Thursday 26 January

Leviticus 8:1–36

Preparing the priests

PREPARE

'But *you* are ... a *royal priesthood*...' (1 Peter 2:9, italics added). Thinking about your daily life, what opportunities are there to perform the role of God's 'royal priesthood'?

READ

Leviticus 8:1–36

EXPLORE

There must have been a growing sense of excitement in Israel. God's dwelling, the Tabernacle ('the tent of meeting'), now stood in the middle of their community. The instructions for the sacrifices required to be 'at one' with God had been spelled out and memorised (chapters 1–7). One thing remained before God himself moved in – the setting apart of a priesthood (Exodus 29:43–46).

Aaron and his family were the designated priests, but since being called, Aaron had taken a leading role in building an idolatrous golden calf (Exodus 32:1–6). Would he now be sidelined? No! Through sacrifice and cleansing, the sinner Aaron could stand in the Holy Place and minister to God (v 30). Good news for all of us!

To perform the role of priest in the Old Testament, Aaron and his sons needed to listen carefully to God so that his instructions could be obeyed; they needed to be willing to serve God at all times and they needed to faithfully walk in God's ways. Put another way, their ears, hands and feet all needed to be fully set apart for God (vs 23,24).

> Then Moses took some of the anointing oil and some of the blood from the altar and sprinkled them on Aaron ... and on his sons ... So he consecrated Aaron ... and his sons...
>
> **Leviticus 8:30**

RESPOND

'Lord, sensitise my ears, to pick up only the frequency of your voice. Sanitise my hands, to be clean of self-interest so that I may serve you and others. Stabilise my feet, to walk carefully in your pathways today. Amen.'

Bible in a year: Exodus 3,4; Matthew 19

Friday 27 January
Leviticus 9:1–24

The point of it all

PREPARE

'To be in your presence / To sit at your feet / Where your love surrounds me / And makes me complete / This is my desire, O Lord / This is my desire' (Noel Richards, 'To Be In Your Presence', 1993)

READ

Leviticus 9:1–24

EXPLORE

In all the details for the sacrifices and the impressive priestly clothing there is a risk that we might lose sight of the point of it all. The ritual is not the point of the ritual! The great promise of the ritual is that it provided the way for the people to enjoy God's welcome as he appeared among them (vs 4,6).

After Aaron had made sacrifices for himself (vs 8–14) and then for all the people (vs 15–21), everything was finally ready. The space between God and his people had been cleared of human sin, so that they could be 'at one' with God (v 7). And then it happened: 'The glory of the LORD appeared to all the people' (v 23). This was no moment for prepared responses: encountering God's presence overwhelmed them, such that they shouted with joy and fell down in awe (v 24).

As Christians we too need to remember that Jesus' ultimate sacrifice was for far more than our forgiveness. Wonderful as that is, his life was given in order to prepare us to know God (John 17:3).

> Moses and Aaron then went into the tent of meeting. When they came out, they blessed the people; and the glory of the LORD appeared to all the people.
>
> **Leviticus 9:23**

RESPOND

What does it mean to you to encounter God? How can you ensure that your 'spiritual practices' become moments of encounter with God?

Bible in a year: Exodus 5,6; Matthew 20

Saturday 28 January

Leviticus 10:1–20

Let God be God

PREPARE

How are your joy levels? Is obedience an issue? Make this prayer your own. 'Restore to me the joy of your salvation and grant me a willing spirit, to sustain me' (Psalm 51:12).

READ

Leviticus 10:1–20

EXPLORE

Coming so soon after the great spiritual high of yesterday's reading, the story of Aaron's eldest sons, Nadab and Abihu, should shock us. God's warm welcome had been experienced by all Israel (9:23), but how quickly the tumultuous shouts of joy (9:24) turned to stunned silence (10:3).

Nadab and Abihu were authorised priests (8:30) and they knew exactly how God required them to approach him: but for some reason they thought they could ignore God's instructions (v 1)! By bringing an unauthorised sacrifice they risked offending God and betraying the people (v 3). This story could make us fearful. Am I 'getting it right' when I approach God? We need have no fear: it is not *our* sacrifice but that of Jesus which opens heaven's door, and his offering is perfect and always accepted (Hebrews 10:14,19–22).

Nadab and Abihu's presumptuous approach to God is contrasted with the apparently unintentional error of Eleazar and Ithamar (vs 16–18). God opposes Nadab and Abihu's pride, but shows understanding towards Aaron's circumstances after their death (vs 19,20). God's mercy triumphs over judgement (James 2:13). Hallelujah!

Aaron's sons Nadab and Abihu took their censers, put fire in them and added incense; and they offered unauthorised fire before the LORD, contrary to his command.

Leviticus 10:1

RESPOND

One of the safeguards against developing 'blind spots' in our relationship with God is to have a close spiritual friend to help us review things. Do you have such a friend? Is it time to meet with them?

Bible in a year: Exodus 7,8; Psalms 13,14

Sunday 29 January
Psalm 80

Are you sleeping, God?

PREPARE

Slowly repeat these words from Psalm 16: 'LORD, you alone are my portion and my cup; you make my lot secure' (Psalm 16:5).

READ

Psalm 80

EXPLORE

When it comes to prayer, God prefers a vat of honesty to a veneer of holiness. In this psalm the Asaphite worship leaders in Jerusalem hurl their frustrations and confusion to God. Don't you remember that we are *your* people (v 1)? Surely you can recall that you saved us from Egypt and planted us in a new land? All the world saw how you caused us to grow and prosper! So how come you've given up on us (v 12)? How long will you ignore our prayers and make us feel bitter and ridiculed (v 6)?

The feelings run deep. The context is the loss of the Northern tribes of Israel (v 2) to Assyrian invasion around 735 BC. The worshippers down south in Jerusalem are shocked at the humiliating desolation of God's own people (v 16).

As we in the western world witness the steady decline in the size, health and influence of the Christian church, are we similarly moved? Can we share in the honest cries of the Asaphites: Restore us (vs 3,7,19)! Wake up and save us (v 2)! Return to us: watch over us and smile on us again (vs 14,19)!

Restore us, O God; make your face shine on us, that we may be saved.

Psalm 80:3

RESPOND

Find a symbol of your nation: perhaps a flag, map or object that sums up your national culture. Hold it before God and pray for the strengthening of God's people in your land.

Bible in a year: Exodus 9,10; Matthew 21

Monday 30 January

Leviticus 11:1–25,44–47

Clean your plate!

PREPARE

Have you ever done a job that left you filthy dirty, or a walk that left you covered in mud? How did it feel to get clean?

READ

Leviticus 11:1–25,44–47

EXPLORE

To enjoy God's welcome in his house, careful attention needed to be shown to Israel's daily diet. The classification of 'clean' and 'unclean' is important because only 'clean' things could be made holy.

The distinction is roughly equivalent to 'normal' and 'unusual', or 'whole' and 'flawed'. In the animal kingdom – animals (vs 2–8,29,30), fish (vs 9–12), birds (vs 13–19), insects (vs 20–23) – some things conform to type, some don't. Fish, for example, that swim 'normally' with fins and scales, are distinguished from 'unusual' water creatures that have neither (vs 9–12).

Many of the reasons are obscure to us, but it seems that the distinction between clean and unclean foods is a parallel to Israel's status as a holy nation (vs 44,45). God had made a distinction between the 'clean' nation of Israel and the other 'unclean' nations that surrounded them. Every time the Israelites ate, they were reminded of their special status and the call to holiness.

In the New Testament age, the distinction between the nations has been abolished (Acts 10:11–28). In Jesus *all* are made clean and may enjoy God's welcome.

'I am the LORD, who brought you up out of Egypt to be your God; therefore be holy, because I am holy.'

Leviticus 11:45

RESPOND

Meditate on this verse: 'A man with leprosy came to him ... "If you are willing, you can make me clean." Jesus ... reached out his hand and touched the man. "I am willing," he said. "Be clean!"' (Mark 1:40,41).

Bible in a year: Exodus 11,12; Matthew 22

Tuesday 31 January
Leviticus 12:1–8

From death to life

PREPARE

Have you ever felt far from God? What or who helped you find your way back?

READ

Leviticus 12:1–8

EXPLORE

Another passage that offers more questions than answers! Childbirth is a good and God-ordained thing (Genesis 1:28), and yet somehow, in ancient Israel, giving birth made the mother unclean (vs 2,5). The remedy was a period of purification. Only when that period had ended could she approach God's house (v 6) and offer her sacrifices, resulting in her becoming clean (vs 7,8).

Why should childbirth make a woman unable to enjoy God's welcome? Some would suggest that God's presence is life and anything that has the shadow of death over it puts it at the opposite end of a spectrum from God himself. Childbirth, with its loss of blood and bodily fluids, appears to bring the mother near to death and thus in the symbolic world of the Old Testament, makes her unclean and far from God.

But there was a way back (vs 7,8), and Jesus' mother herself fulfilled these acts of ritual purification (Luke 2:22–24). How wonderful though that Mary's son abolished them altogether! He could touch a bleeding woman and even a dead child, and directly transmit healing and life (Luke 8:40–56). No temple needed, just a touch.

'…"A woman who becomes pregnant and gives birth to a son will be ceremonially unclean for seven days …"'

Leviticus 12:2

RESPOND

Do you know someone who needs a healing, life-giving touch from Jesus? Or perhaps someone who feels that they have made so many mistakes that there is no way back to God for them? Pray for Jesus to touch them now.

Bible in a year: Exodus 13,14; Matthew 23

Wednesday 1 February
Leviticus 13:1–11,45,46

Sore losers?

PREPARE

Quieten yourself and pray: 'Jesus, lead me to the Father's embrace; Father, breathe on me your Holy Spirit; Spirit, empower me to follow Jesus today.'

READ

Leviticus 13:1–11,45,46

EXPLORE

In Leviticus, holiness is shown in 'wholeness' and consequently only whole people or things can approach a holy God.

In this chapter, the same Hebrew word (*tzaraat*) is used to describe skin diseases (v 2), and mould on clothing (v 47). Later on it's also used for mildew on the walls of the houses (14:34,35). It seems that this 'umbrella word' embraces much more than the skin conditions (eczema? psoriasis?) described in today's reading. It seems to denote a lack or loss of wholeness in the person or item afflicted.

Those diseases which were deep seated and long-lasting identified the person – or the mouldy clothing – as unclean (eg vs 7,8,51). The clothing had to be burned (v 52) and the person banished from society (v 46). There was no hope for them unless – and until – their disease cleared up and they became whole again.

No hope... until, centuries later, one such banished man experienced the welcome and healing power of Jesus (Luke 5:12–14). God himself, in the form of his Son, approached an outcast leper and shockingly brought God's welcome to him. God is still reaching out to hopeless sufferers today!

'As long as they have the disease they remain unclean. They must live alone; they must live outside the camp.'

Leviticus 13:46

RESPOND

Who are the 'sore losers' in your community – those who have been ostracised because of how people perceive them? What might you be able to do to show them the welcome of Jesus?

Bible in a year: Exodus 15,16; Psalms 15,16

Radical remedies

PREPARE

Reflect on this question: 'Who am I when no one else is watching?'

READ

Leviticus 14:33–57

EXPLORE

Today's reading looks forward to the time when Israel will live in houses in Canaan (v 34). What if a spreading mould should appear there? Well, given that it is at home, no one need know... but ignoring the mould could cause clothing to be infected (13:47–52), and then, perhaps the skin itself may become unclean (13:1–46). Beyond that lies a world of pain, social stigma and separation from God's house.

Better by far to deal with things before they get worse. Admit you've got a problem and ask the priest to come and inspect it (v 35). If it's not just a surface issue, but appears to be going deep into the fabric of your home (v 37), and if it persists, then action is needed (v 40). The risks associated with household contamination are so great that ultimately the house itself may need to be destroyed (v 45).

It is tempting to ignore personal flaws that – like the mould at home – are not known to others. But the risk is that they develop into something that becomes a major pollutant in our lives with God. As Jesus counselled, better to take radical action than risk private sin developing into something far worse (Matthew 5:27–30).

'It must be torn down – its stones, timbers and all the plaster – and taken out of the town to an unclean place.'

Leviticus 14:45

RESPOND

'Search me, God ... See if there is any offensive way in me, and lead me in the way everlasting' (Psalm 139:23,24). Is the Holy Spirit showing you any 'stones' that you need to throw away?

Bible in a year: Exodus 17,18; Matthew 24

Friday 3 February

Leviticus 15:1–33

Mind the gap!

PREPARE

'I praise you because I am fearfully and wonderfully made; your works are wonderful…' (Psalm 139:14). Take time to thank God for your body and rededicate it to his service.

READ

Leviticus 15:1–33

EXPLORE

No one can accuse the Bible of being prudish! Various kinds of male and female bodily fluids are described as causes of uncleanness. Remedies are given for becoming clean again, including washing and offering sacrifices (vs 13–15,28–30).

Sex, semen and periods (vs 16–19) are very 'earthy' – God's gifts for the survival of the human race. And perhaps that is the point. It's not that they are sinful, but that they are symbolic of our physicality and mortality – our very humanness. These laws reminded the Israelites just how different they were from God, and how attentive they needed to be to that chasm as they approached him in worship.

In the Old Testament world, that chasm was bridged by laws and ritual, generously given to human beings by God. Our access as Christians is now secured by the cleansing of Jesus. Our challenge today is not in making our humanity acceptable to God (Jesus has done that), but rather in remembering how big a gap Jesus has spanned for us – and how holy is the God who welcomes us (Hebrews 10:19–22).

'You must keep the Israelites separate from things that make them unclean, so they will not die in their uncleanness for defiling my dwelling-place, which is among them.'

Leviticus 15:31

RESPOND

Turn the words of this old hymn into your prayer: 'Oh, the love that drew salvation's plan! Oh, the grace that brought it down to man! Oh, the mighty gulf that God did span, At Calvary!' (William R Newell, 1895).

Bible in a year: Exodus 19,20; Matthew 25

Scripture Union
DIARY OF A DISCIPLE
LUKE'S STORY
HOLIDAY CLUB
INCLUDES
PHOTOCOPIABLE RESOURCES AND FREE EXTRAS ONLINE

WAY IN

1 and 2 Thessalonians

Walking worthily

About the writer
Ben Green

Ben is married to Jess, and they live in Birmingham, where he is vicar of Christ Church Selly Park and she is a doctor. When he isn't vicaring, Ben is most likely to be found writing computer software, but he also enjoys walking up (real) mountains, playing the piano and letting Jess plan their holidays.

Paul had a torrid time in and around Thessalonica (Acts 17:1–15). He preached the gospel in the synagogue and saw a large number of converts. But after about three weeks the persecution started: a handful of jealous Jews formed a mob, which started a riot and ended with Paul and Silas running away by night, forced to leave the believers to fend for themselves.

The Church had an explosive start. It's a miracle it survived, which helps explain the depth of Paul's love for them. He warned them of persecution, but I doubt even he expected it to come so quickly. The circumstances caused Paul to lay bare in these letters his pastoral heart: a twin commitment to God's Word and God's people.

They had responded quickly to the gospel but their faith wasn't shallow: it was genuine and life-changing. The adversity they faced from the beginning produced in them such love for one another that Paul can't stop talking about it. The tone of these letters suggests Paul wished he could have spent longer with them.

Look out for how Paul urges them to keep doing 'more and more' what they are already doing, to continue in what they've started. For Paul, the Christian life means learning to walk in a way that pleases God and is worthy of his call. It means growing in holiness. The Thessalonians had made a good start in difficult circumstances – but would they keep walking?

Saturday 4 February
1 Thessalonians 1:1–10

For all, our thanks

PREPARE

Paul begins each of his letters praying for peace – in the Bible that's more about wholeness and completeness than the absence of conflict. Whatever storms you are facing, take a breath and ask God to fill you with his peace.

READ

1 Thessalonians 1:1–10

EXPLORE

After his customary greeting (v 1), Paul shows the depth and warmth of his love for the Thessalonians. Have a look at what he gives thanks for (vs 2,3). Notice how Paul's thanksgiving is grounded in things they do: their work (of faith), their labour (of love) and their endurance (in hope). The reality of their faith, love and hope is proved by what they do.

He carries on in the same vein: the gospel message came not only with words but with power (v 5); they turned away from their old life and began to live differently (vs 6,9); they became visible examples of faith (v 8). As Jesus said (in Matthew 7:16), 'By their fruit you will recognise them.' I wonder what people would recognise from the fruit of your lifestyle, and mine?

One final point is important: did they do this to earn God's love? No, for that is where Paul begins (v 4). God *first* loves and chooses his people; *then* his people respond, hopefully as wholeheartedly as in first-century Thessalonica.

We always thank God for all of you.

1 Thessalonians 1:2

RESPOND

How can you give thanks for your Christian family? What is the good that you can say thank you for – especially when it comes to those you find difficult? Ask God to help you see, and then spend time in prayer saying thank you.

Bible in a year: Exodus 21,22; Psalm 17

Sunday 5 February

Psalm 81

Joy in the Lord

PREPARE

What has God done for you? Beyond the gift of life in Jesus and the Spirit – what has God done for you, in your life? What difference has he made?

READ

Psalm 81

EXPLORE

Verses 1 and 2 make a great introduction to a service of praise and worship – maybe even for your service today! But what if 'joy' is the very last thing you feel in your heart? In this psalm, making joyful music comes not from emotion but willing obedience: it is a 'decree', an 'ordinance', a 'statute' (vs 4,5). But how can God *command* us to be joyful?

In the Bible joy has an object: God. And it is closely linked with the thankfulness of remembrance (vs 7–10). Biblical joy begins not with emotion but with *choosing* to rejoice in what God has done for us, no matter how we feel right now. Thank God, his gift of life depends not on how we feel day-to-day, but on what he has already done.

When I find myself in a funk, it is nearly always down to my stubborn heart (v 12). In those times, joy seems impossible to find. The answer? To listen, and to follow what God (and I) know is best for me (v 13). Oh, that it were as easy to do as to say!

Sing for joy to God our strength.

Psalm 81:1

RESPOND

However you feel today, can you rejoice in what God has done for you? If you're finding it a challenge, try to listen to the words of Scripture – listen and follow them into the heart of God's love for you.

Bible in a year: Exodus 23,24; Matthew 26

Monday 6 February
1 Thessalonians 2:1–12

A sea of troubles

PREPARE

I hope you have never been treated as badly as Paul was. But what troubles *are* you facing? What persecution for your faith do you see in your daily life?

READ

1 Thessalonians 2:1–12

EXPLORE

Paul continued his mission despite being in physical danger almost everywhere he went (v 2). Yet passages like this suggest that what hurt – more than very real sticks and stones – were the words and false accusations he faced from the churches he planted. Read verses 3 to 6 and 9 again. What do you think Paul had been accused of by the way he responds?

'You know,' he says (vs 1,2,5,11); 'Surely you remember' (v 9); 'You are witnesses' (v 10). He counters the accusations by reminding them of the truth: that he loved them (vs 7,8) and worked hard not to be a burden, so he could offer the gospel free of charge (v 9). As the Thessalonians' love was proved by their actions, so was Paul's.

Look again over the passage to see the different familial phrases and pictures Paul uses. His motivation was to build God's family, which is why he kept going despite everything, why his love was so passionate – and why the hurt cut so deep.

Just as a nursing mother cares for her children, so we cared for you.

1 Thessalonians 2:7,8

RESPOND

Paul and his companions gave everything; they were willing to suffer terribly – physically and emotionally – for the sake of sharing the gospel. Is there a situation where you would love to share the gospel, but too often give in to your fear and stay silent?

Bible in a year: Exodus 25,26; Matthew 27

Tuesday 7 February

1 Thessalonians 2:13–20

Slings and arrows

PREPARE

When you share stories or testimonies of God at work in your life, are they usually about God's provision, or healing, or gifts? In other words, are they always positive?

READ

1 Thessalonians 2:13–20

EXPLORE

Paul can't shut up about God and Jesus! Although he often talks about 'my (or our) gospel' (eg 1:5), ultimately, he knows it is God's message (v 13; see also 1:8; 2:2). It has a power and a life of its own, working within the lives of those who believe (v 13). In the Thessalonians it formed a family likeness as they imitated people they'd never met (v 14).

But what did that imitation look like? Read verse 14.

Paul was open about the suffering he and they were facing. But too often Christians hide our personal hardships and struggles, making it harder for others to be open and honest with us about theirs.

At this point in Paul's life his troubles were almost entirely caused by Jews (eg Acts 17:13). He was hurt and angry at being rejected by his own people. His language condemning them sounds like the Old Testament prophets. But more than that, he was angry at those who forced him to abandon an infant church, which was now suffering and in grave danger.

> You suffered from your own people.
>
> **1 Thessalonians 2:14**

RESPOND

Are you willing to imitate the early churches in Judea and Thessalonica in their suffering (v 14)? How can you be more honest – with yourself and with others – about your struggles, so together you can draw on God's strength to persevere?

Bible in a year: Exodus 27,28; Matthew 28

Wednesday 8 February
1 Thessalonians 3:1–13

Little fears grow great

PREPARE

It's easy to tell when I'm worried because I start shallow-breathing. Do you have a similar 'tell'? What is it that makes you anxious? What are you afraid of, or concerned about?

READ

1 Thessalonians 3:1–13

EXPLORE

'Where little fears grow great, great love grows there.' Thus speaks the Player Queen in Shakespeare's *Hamlet*. It is in Paul's anxiety for the church in Thessalonica that we see the depth of his love.

As we saw in the Way In, Paul had spent barely any time in Thessalonica before he was forced to flee. Many had responded quickly and eagerly to the gospel – but what would become of them now? Would they be 'unsettled' by their 'trials' (v 3) or 'tempted' (v 5) to take the easy route out of persecution and reject the gospel?

Thankfully the answer was a resounding 'No!' Can you feel Paul's emotion? When he received a good report from Timothy, he wasn't simply glad. 'Now we really live,' he says (v 8). He'd been 'worried to death', as we might put it today.

Paul wasn't interested in making converts. He cared about making disciples, people learning to live as followers of Jesus, standing firm in God (v 8), increasing and overflowing in love (v 12), made strong, blameless and holy by God (v 13).

For now we really live, since you are standing firm in the Lord.

1 Thessalonians 3:8

RESPOND

For Paul, conversion wasn't the goal. Like putting your boots on, it was simply the beginning of the walk. How has your walk gone since you put your faith boots on? Give thanks to God for the places he has walked with you so far.

Bible in a year: Exodus 29,30; Psalm 18

Thursday 9 February

1 Thessalonians 4:1–12

Do as you please?

PREPARE

Think of something you've done that was really hard work, or that took a long time, or that required a lot of effort. What kept you going? Was it worth it in the end?

READ

1 Thessalonians 4:1–12

EXPLORE

I am a useless long-distance runner. I can manage an occasional sprint, but that's it. However, I love walking, particularly up mountains. I have a theory that the best views are only accessible by foot.

Most translations use 'live' in verse 1, but the word Paul uses is 'walk'. The Christian life is not a sprint. It is not even a marathon. It is a long, steady walk into holiness (v 7). That may be why it's easy to be distracted, especially by the bright lights and seductive temptations of sexual immorality (vs 3–6). Then (and now), Paul's teaching on sexuality was counter-cultural: he says God's people must not indulge their desires and let them rule over them, but learn self-control and holiness instead (vs 4,5).

The Christian walk is not complicated but it's hard. From controlling our passions to learning to love one another, it takes daily effort – which is why Paul says, 'do so more and more' (v 10). It's hard work but the view will be worth it.

For God did not call us to be impure, but to live a holy life.

1 Thessalonians 4:7

RESPOND

Do you assess your behaviour, speech, thoughts and feelings to help you live to please God (v 1)? Including when it comes to sex? Ask God to show you what you need to do or avoid, to help you grow in holiness.

Bible in a year: Exodus 31,32; Acts 1

Friday 10 February
1 Thessalonians 4:13–18

To die, to sleep

PREPARE

Give thanks for those you have known and loved who have 'fallen asleep in [Jesus]' (v 14). Thank God for their example and their encouragement.

READ

1 Thessalonians 4:13–18

EXPLORE

We learn much about Paul's pastoral heart in this passage. First, he wants to deal with ignorance (v 13), which causes many issues in the Christian walk. How do you deal with your own ignorance in matters of faith? *Do* you?

Second, he meets their concern with the central message of the gospel: 'Jesus died and rose again' (v 14). Notice we '*sleep* in death', but Jesus '*died*': he endured death and its consequences which means that for his followers it is more like sleep.

Third, Paul's confidence in Jesus' return comes from 'the Lord's word' (v 15). This is not made up by Paul, but the truth from the only one we can truly trust. The picture he uses is of an important visitor being greeted and then welcomed into a city by its citizens (vs 16,17). It will be a wonderful reunion.

Fourth, we don't know everything about the future (see 5:1), but we know enough to 'encourage one another' (v 18). Pastoral care and encouragement is for *all* of us to practise.

For we believe that Jesus died and rose again.

1 Thessalonians 4:14

RESPOND

How can you encourage someone in your church family this week? Whether they are bereaved or not, how can you (gently) encourage them with the truth of the gospel? How can you go out of your way to show them they are loved?

Bible in a year: Exodus 33,34; Acts 2

Saturday 11 February

1 Thessalonians 5:1–11

Day and night

PREPARE

Bring to mind the most spectacular sunset (or sunrise if you like to get up early) that you've ever seen. Give thanks for the light, the warmth, the power, the life that the sun brings to all.

READ

1 Thessalonians 5:1–11

EXPLORE

Did you spot how many metaphors Paul mixes here? He begins with the 'day of the Lord' which is like a 'thief' (v 2), an invasion (v 3) and 'labour' (v 3). Like the disciples before them (Acts 1:6,7), the Thessalonians wanted to know when this day would come. I can sympathise – I like to know 'when' so I can plan!

Paul's answer is that we don't *need* to know; we need to be *ready*. The 'day of the Lord' will come – but the day of God's kingdom has already dawned. Once again Paul returns to the gospel: 'he died for us so that … we may live together with him' (v 10). Don't worry about when Jesus will return, Paul says, but learn to live the life he has won for you (v 8).

Again he urges them to 'encourage one another' (v 11; 4:18). Why? Because keeping focus is hard! We need to remind one another of the truth, uphold one another as we walk and help one another face the light.

> You are all children of the light and children of the day.
>
> **1 Thessalonians 5:5**

RESPOND

The contrast between living in the darkness and living in the light is stark. Ask God to show you where your lifestyle and behaviour belong to the night, so you can turn away from it, and instead live in the light of Jesus' day.

Bible in a year: Exodus 35,36; Psalm 19

Sunday 12 February
Psalm 82

This is God!

PREPARE

Do you ever wonder what you would do, what decisions you would make, if you were 'in charge'? What would you change? What wrongs would you right?

READ

Psalm 82

EXPLORE

Who do you think are the 'gods' that Asaph rails against in this psalm? Pagan idols? The 'rulers' and 'authorities' Paul describes in Ephesians 6:12? Human rulers with authority?

To me the clue is in verse 1, which talks about God presiding over the 'great assembly'. The word is used throughout Exodus and Numbers to describe the whole people of Israel. That means the 'gods' (vs 1,5,6), the 'sons of the Most High' (v 6), are *all* God's people, called and set apart to be different, to behave differently from the world.

There is no escape for us from verses 2 to 4. *All* God's people are required to bring God's rule and justice to the world. *All* God's people must have the same heart, the same concerns as God for the 'weak and the fatherless', the 'poor and the oppressed', the 'needy' (vs 3,4).

God will one day bring the perfect justice his people are supposed to bring – the question is, on which side of God's justice will we be standing? And what are we doing about it here and now?

Rise up, O God.

Psalm 82:8

RESPOND

Do you share God's heart for justice? Or is your faith more about believing the right things? Both are vital, but most of us are stronger in one than the other. Ask God to help you keep the right balance between them in your faith.

Bible in a year: Exodus 37,38; Acts 3

Monday 13 February

1 Thessalonians 5:12–28

In good faith

PREPARE

What would a perfect church look like (the family of people, not the building)? What would it do (or not do)? How would the people act?

READ

1 Thessalonians 5:12–28

EXPLORE

I'm not an expert on first-century paper, but it feels like Paul was running out of it here! His final instructions come tumbling out one after another. Which jumped out at you when you read through them all?

Four times in these verses Paul addresses them as 'brothers and sisters' (vs 12,14,25,27). This is a family of faith, with all the joys and challenges that brings. The church in Thessalonica was certainly not perfect (v 14), but Paul makes harmonious life the responsibility of everyone (not simply the elders).

What do you make of verses 16–18? What does it mean to rejoice, pray and give thanks no matter what? When awful things happen, how can we give thanks? When we're finding it hard to get up in the morning, how can we rejoice?

It helps to recognise how circumstances and our attitude can 'quench' the life and gifts of the Spirit (v 19) as we hold on to evil and let go of good. Hard though it is, sometimes we have to be deliberate about doing the opposite (vs 21,22).

The one who calls you is faithful, and he will do it.

1 Thessalonians 5:24

RESPOND

I love Paul's final prayer (vs 23,24). Ultimately all we have, are and will be rests on God's faithfulness, not our own. Picture your church family – even those you find difficult – and pray these words over them: even rejoice in them.

Bible in a year: Exodus 39,40; Acts 4

Tuesday 14 February

2 Thessalonians 1:1–12

According to their deserts

PREPARE

Do you keep a prayer journal, to keep track of what you pray and the way God answers? If you do, have a look back at some answered prayer. If you don't, how might you do this?

READ

2 Thessalonians 1:1–12

EXPLORE

I had a decision to make: should I accept the offer of the perfect and highly paid job? I was desperate for God to say 'yes', but his answer was 'no', that I should stay put. It took two years before I understood and could give thanks (and mean it!).

Paul gives thanks (v 3) that his prayers have been answered (see 1 Thessalonians 3:12) – all the more amazing because they were suffering (vs 4,5). It sounds serious. Paul describes what was happening as 'persecutions', 'trials', 'suffering' and 'trouble'. It was bad.

This helps explain the language Paul uses next. Note when the punishment will come (v 7) and who will receive it (v 8). The word means paying a penalty, facing consequences and just deserts, not something over the top or arbitrary.

Also note the difference between the punishment (v 9) and Paul's prayer (v 12): to be cut off from God is the ultimate consequence of sin; to be with him and in him is the greatest reward.

Your faith is growing more and more, and the love all of you have for one another is increasing.

2 Thessalonians 1:3

RESPOND

How are you struggling or suffering at the moment? Can you pray some of Paul's prayers (for example, vs 3,11,12)? Ask God to give you the eyes of faith to see things as he does, to know his presence more and more.

Bible in a year: Leviticus 1–3; Acts 5

Wednesday 15 February

2 Thessalonians 2:1–12

Breath of life

PREPARE

How do you rebel against God and ignore or reject his teachings? How have you fallen short already today? Make a note of them (you'll need that for a time of confession later).

READ

2 Thessalonians 2:1–12

EXPLORE

There are few passages in Paul's letters more difficult than this one, not least because his argument refers to teachings we don't have (vs 5,6). While we can't understand in full, we can discern some important truths and warnings.

First, sin is rebellion against God – lawlessness, chaos (v 3) – which tries to take his place (v 4). Second, the full expression of sin's rebellion is being held back (v 6) – perhaps by God himself, perhaps by the rule of law. Third, Satan works through powerful deception and lies (v 9). Fourth, God's judgement is to give those who reject his truth exactly what they want (vs 10–12). And fifth, although these patterns of sin are repeated throughout history, one day someone will arise as the ultimate expression of this rebellion. But how will God deal with him? Read verse 8.

There is not even a skirmish, let alone a great battle. Take a breath and breathe out – that is all Jesus needs to do to 'overthrow' this enemy!

Don't let anyone deceive you in any way.

2 Thessalonians 2:3

RESPOND

Pick up the list of things you need to confess that you noted earlier. For each one, take a deep breath (breathing in God's grace and power), and then breathe out slowly (breathing out God's praise and victory over sin). Finally pray, 'Thank you!'

Bible in a year: Leviticus 4,5; Psalms 20,21

With all my heart

PREPARE

Who are the people you love most? Whether friends or family, picture them, give thanks for them, and pray God would bless, encourage, and strengthen them.

READ

2 Thessalonians 2:13 – 3:3

EXPLORE

Paul can't help himself – he returns again to thanksgiving (2:13). Have you grasped the depth of his love and heartfelt thanks for the Thessalonians yet?

The end of chapter 2 is rich and beautiful. First, our salvation is from beginning to end the work of God who loves us (2:13). Second, that salvation is worked out in us in a partnership between the Spirit and ourselves (2:13,15). Third, the call to this glorious life with Jesus comes through the gospel (2:14). Fourth, the Christian walk is not easy, so we need God's grace and constant encouragement (2:16).

I wonder how many times we stop there. It is all too easy for churches to be rich in words but poor in deeds (and of course the opposite). But for Paul the two go together: we must be strong in 'every good deed *and* word' (2:17). When churches get that balance right, the gospel does indeed 'spread rapidly' and is 'honoured' (3:1). Why? Because people see our actions living up to what we say.

What mission activities are you and your church involved in? How could you not only pray, but also help to ensure that those activities involve spreading *and* honouring the gospel?

... brothers and sisters loved by the Lord.

2 Thessalonians 2:13

RESPOND

Pray Paul's prayer, trusting and rejoicing in God's faithfulness and protection (vs 1–3).

Bible in a year: Leviticus 6,7; Acts 6

Friday 17 February

2 Thessalonians 3:4–18

Actions fair and good

PREPARE

Are you tired? Weary of the daily struggle? Ask God to direct your heart into his love. Picture yourself surrounded and held by the loving arms of your heavenly Father God (v 16).

READ

2 Thessalonians 3:4–18

EXPLORE

The Christian walk is a daily effort. We don't walk for a couple of hours and then arrive; we continue walking (v 4). It sounds easy to keep God's love as our beginning and end, but the lure of other things means it isn't. Hence Paul's prayer for perseverance (v 5).

Have you ever been involved in church discipline, either giving or receiving it? It's so difficult to get right that many churches shy away from it. But Paul had a high view of the church as a community and family, and he knew how critical its members' behaviour is for its reputation with outsiders.

Paul also knew how dangerous disruptive behaviour and disobedience can be (v 6). They spread through a community like cancer, eating away at the heart, killing the roots. They need to be challenged, but carefully and graciously. We need to be careful not to treat our Christian brothers and sisters as the enemy (v 15). For, even as he warns those who are idle and disruptive (vs 11,12), he includes *all* the family in his final prayers (vs 16,18).

Never tire of doing what is good.

2 Thessalonians 3:13

RESPOND

Do you need to hear Paul's warnings? How can you be a good example to your Christian brothers and sisters, as Paul was (vs 8,9)? Pray God would fill you to overflowing with his peace and his grace.

Bible in a year: Leviticus 8,9; Acts 7

WAY IN

Hosea 1–14

Faithful God

These were troubled, uncertain times. Towards the end of the eighth century BC, the kingdoms of Judah and, more immediately, Israel, were facing meltdown. Economic and political troubles rumbled on, but the fundamental issue was their unfaithfulness to God. In Israel there was a mishmash of idolatry (Baals) alongside nominal lip-service to their one true God. It seemed as if everyone went after whatever suited them best – and this included embracing the promiscuity accepted in their idol-worshipping culture. Not so different from our lives today then? Judgement was coming. The superpower of Assyria would soon come 'down like the wolf on the fold'* and Israel would be carried off into exile (722 BC); Judah's fate would follow later in 597 BC at the hands of the Babylonians.

Hosea's message (told through his marriage to a prostitute) was not an easy one. Yet his own name spoke of the grace of his loving God – 'God has delivered'. His whole life was to be a picture both of God's judgement of his people's unfaithfulness, but also of his saving love for them. In the end, there is a call to repentance and a promise of forgiveness, restoration, renewed flourishing and security as the people choose again to live in the shelter of their God. 'I will heal ... and love them ... answer ... and care' (Hosea 14:4–8). For us too there is hope – whatever the darkness and challenges of our time – as we faithfully 'dwell again in his shade' (Hosea 14:7).

About the writer
'Tricia Williams

'Tricia worked with Scripture Union for many years, developing and editing Bible resources. In recent years she has been researching and writing about faith and dementia. She and her husband Emlyn live in Norfolk, where they are part of a local Anglican church.

*Lord Byron, 'Destruction of Sennacherib', 1815

Forgotten God?

PREPARE

What gets in the way of your relationship with God? Take time to allow God's Spirit to draw you back into his embrace.

READ

Hosea 1:1 – 2:13

EXPLORE

Other prophets had used images of infidelity (Isaiah, Jeremiah, Ezekiel), but God asks Hosea to go further. He is to become the living example of God's own painful experience of his people turning from him. Hosea's story is the backdrop for God's message.

The 'word' came to Hosea to go and marry – not a girl from a faithful, God-honouring family, but a prostitute, depicting the unfaithfulness of God's people (1:2). God would teach his prophet through his own bitter experience (1:2–8). The names of Hosea's children (or at least, those of Gomer, his wife) spoke of God's judgement. Questions of friends and relatives about names for the children would bring surprising answers (1:4,5,6,9). But to Hosea, God whispers the promise of their reversal: you will be my people; you are loved (1:10 – 2:1).

Out of this living picture, God speaks his judgement of unfaithful Israel (2:1–13).

As we read, we can imagine Hosea's distress as he responds to the behaviour of Gomer. She has run after other men, resulting in 'children of adultery' (2:4), not been grateful for the gifts of her husband (2:8), wasting these in worship of Baal (2:8). God draws out his application: Israel's extravagant, unfaithful behaviour *will* be stopped. They have forgotten him, but...

'... she burned incense to the Baals ... and went after lovers, but me she forgot,' declares the LORD.

Hosea 2:13

RESPOND

Have we forgotten God? Misused his gifts? Repent and receive renewed assurance that you are his and are loved (2:1).

Bible in a year: Leviticus 10–12; Psalm 22

Sunday 19 February

Psalm 83

God, Most High

PREPARE

Reflect on your world and its problems. Cry out to God with his people through time: 'O God, do not remain silent...' (Psalm 83:1).

READ

Psalm 83

EXPLORE

Sometimes, as God's people, we feel under threat by forces in our world which don't honour God and seem to hate those who do. Songwriter Asaph, in earlier times than Hosea's, writes this communal song of lament. God's cherished people are threatened by jealous enemies, and this psalm gives them words to express their prayers (vs 1–4).

The target of their enemies' destructive hatred isn't just God's people, but God himself ('against you', verse 5). Tracking back through their history, the psalmist recalls those who have turned against God's chosen people (eg Edomites, the Ishmaelites*), now joined by Assyria (v 8). He reminds them of God's victories over their enemies in the past, calling on God to act again, to save them (vs 9–12). Overwhelmed by the state of the world which seems to teeter on the edge, here God's people find encouragement to call on their God ('my God,' v 13) to defeat their enemies again and blow evil forces away. But notice that even in their call for judgement, there is mercy and purpose: 'so that they will seek your name' (v 16).

Who are the enemies of God and our faith today? How might we join with others to lament, and to pray for ourselves and them?

*Genesis 36; Genesis 16

> Let them know that you, whose name is the LORD – that you alone are the Most High over all the earth.
>
> **Psalm 83:18**

RESPOND

Do that now, remembering how God has worked in the lives of his people in the past.

Bible in a year: Leviticus 13,14; Acts 8

Monday 20 February
Hosea 2:14 – 3:5

God who loves

PREPARE

Difficult times? Yet, how has trouble ('the Valley of Achor', 2:15) sometimes brought you glimmers of hope and renewed awareness of God's love?

READ

Hosea 2:14 – 3:5

EXPLORE

Judgement of Israel would be radical, but God is a faithful lover. When his beloved is hopeless and empty, he courts her tenderly, leading her to a new place of blessing (vs 14,15). Turning to her husband again will bring freedom from the tyranny of false idols (vs 16,17). Harmony will be restored. In mutual agreement, there will be righteousness, justice, love and compassion – and the betrothed 'will acknowledge the LORD' (vs 19,20). Abundant growth follows – the result of God's planting (v 23). The upside-down ways of God turn 'not loved' into the discovery of being loved and of being his people. Then they will freely assert, 'You are my God' (v 23). Perhaps you can recall such a pattern in your own life.

Still in the opening 'chapter' of Hosea's prophetic, symbolic story, there is one more scene to play out. He proactively seeks out his adulterous wife, pays the price for her and takes her home (3:1–3). God helps Hosea understand. Bereft of leadership and spiritual direction, the Israelites *will* eventually 'seek the LORD' again (vs 4,5). Recognising their own unworthiness, they know that in God blessing awaits.

'I will show my love to the one I called "Not my loved one". I will say to those called "Not my people", "You are my people"; and they will say, "You are my God."'

Hosea 2:23

RESPOND

'Oh, the love that sought me! Oh, the blood that bought me!' (William Spencer Walton, 1850–1906). Praise God for loving you, seeking you and paying the price for your redemption in Jesus.

Bible in a year: Leviticus 15,16; Acts 9

Tuesday 21 February

Hosea 4:1 – 5:7

Unfaithful people

PREPARE

Reflect on areas of your life where you have been unfaithful to God. Bring them to God now, asking for his forgiveness and help to put things right.

READ

Hosea 4:1 – 5:7

EXPLORE

God has drawn his picture through the life and bitter experience of Hosea. Now the prophet speaks out its message: 'no faithfulness, no love, no acknowledgment of God' (4:1). The people and their leaders 'stumble' about (4:5), having 'exchanged their glorious God for something disgraceful' (4:7). Idolatry and sexual immorality do not bring flourishing, but dissatisfaction (v 10) and judgement (5:1). Before cringing at the doom and gloom of these Old Testament words, think about your own society, and descriptions here which might fit today.

It's tempting to blame those at the sharp end of failure (prostitutes, petty criminals or refugees making illegal journeys), yet God's words challenge us to question *whose* actions or inaction have allowed such situations (4:14). Have we unwittingly collaborated in such behaviour? Let's pray for understanding (4:14).

The Lord longs to care for his people, but persistent, deliberate, sinful behaviour means they are unable to receive the blessings of his love: 'their rulers dearly love shameful ways' (v 18; 5:6,7). Judgement and punishment are coming and, in a way, in our own sinful world too, that is good news. As you read on, remember the end of Hosea's story (2:21; 3:5).

> ... the LORD has a charge to bring against you ... 'There is no faithfulness, no love, no acknowledgment of God in the land.'
>
> **Hosea 4:1**

RESPOND

Pray for the world and your local community. Pray that people and leaders will listen to God's voice, and that you will be faithful in speaking out his truth.

Bible in a year: Leviticus 17,18; Acts 10

Moving the boundaries...

PREPARE

Take time to 'earnestly' seek God now (Hosea 5:15).

READ

Hosea 5:8 – 6:11a

EXPLORE

For Israel (signified by Ephraim here, 5:9), punishment is on its way. The people consort with their godless enemy, Assyria (v 13) – but there is no easy cure-all there. Although Judah's leaders try to shift the boundaries (5:10), it hasn't escaped God's notice. Judgement will follow for them too. The rot has already set in (v 12). God's repeated calls to return to him are ignored, and now his people have chosen a miserable outcome (v 15). But notice the hints of hope: until they 'seek my face' (v 15).

Watch out for the possible double meanings in chapter 6:1–3. Are these beautiful, prophetic words of restoration, even pointing to Christ's resurrection (v 2)? Or are they words of sardonic reproof to those who take God's love and forgiveness for granted (see also Psalm 78:36,37)? Either (or both) might be the case, but here in Hosea's message the result is God's exasperated rebuke: 'What can I do with you?' and a reminder that his judgement is also as certain as sunrise (vs 3,5). Good-sounding words and religious practice don't account for broken covenant, violence and unfaithfulness: God desires our true acknowledgement (vs 6,7). He sees us (v 10). And Judah? A time of reckoning ('harvest') is coming for them too (6:11).

'For I desire mercy,
not sacrifice, and
acknowledgment of God
rather than burnt offerings.'

Hosea 6:6

RESPOND

Do we sometimes persist with our own ways, assuming that outward appearances will get God's approval? Ask God to help you worship him in truth as you seek to live for him today.

Bible in a year: Leviticus 19,20; Psalms 23,24

Thursday 23 February

Hosea 6:11b – 7:16

A God who longs...

PREPARE

Cry out to God, bringing to him whatever is troubling you now. He longs to hear you.

READ

Hosea 6:11b – 7:16

EXPLORE

The people of Israel are in deep trouble. Things are not going well. Why doesn't God do something about it? Here is God's own lament over his people.

God wants to make things right (6:11 – 7:1), to heal his people, but like silly birds (doves, 7:11), they look in the wrong directions for help. Senseless evildoing engulfs them, and they forget that God sees all (vs 1,2). Their leaders (eg Jeroboam II, 2 Kings 14) encourage and approve their wickedness, adultery and drunkenness. The rulers' examples will backfire, bringing them failure too (v 7). Arrogant compromise leaves the Israelites like half-baked bread – uncooked on one side, burned on the other – useless (v 8). Stupidly, ignoring God, they fail to realise that those they approach for help (v 11) will exploit and use them (vs 9,10).

God longs to rescue them (v 13), but caught in a trap of their own making (vs 12,13), the people squander their hope in God. Indulging in self-pity, they rebel and speak about him untruthfully. Looking in the wrong places for help, they turn away from God (v 14). He has provided good resources, but they have not looked after what he has given (vs 15,16). Insolent words will result in their own downfall and ridicule. Yet, God longs to heal his people.

'I long to redeem them but they speak about me falsely. They do not cry out to me from their hearts but wail on their beds.'

Hosea 7:13,14

RESPOND

Pause, reflect, lament. Speak out the longings of your heart – for yourself, your family, the church, your nation, this world.

Bible in a year: Leviticus 21,22; Acts 11

Friday 24 February

Hosea 8:1 – 9:9

Broken idols

PREPARE

How are people in your country (community, church) being hurt because they have put something/someone else in God's place? Pray for them.

READ

Hosea 8:1 – 9:9

EXPLORE

People *say* that they acknowledge God. But their lives tell a different story (8:1–4). God's ways are rejected. Self rules, and people choose their own priorities without consulting God. They regard silver and gold as their own, turning it into their gods (8:6). What parallels do we see in our own societies? Even, perhaps, in our churches? Such behaviour brings brokenness and failure. It isn't just that God is angry with their faithlessness; they are responsible themselves for the degradation and want in which they find themselves (8:7–9).

They've sown the wind; now comes the whirlwind (8:7) – defeat, oppression and ignominy. Like a prostitute, God's people have sold themselves (8:9). Their many altars are not signs of repentance, but are caught up in the sinful practices of idolatrous culture (8:11). God's own words and laws are foreign to them (8:12). They have forgotten their Maker – but God remembers their sin (8:13,14).

Unfaithfulness to him brings its own punishment. The wages of 'prostitution' do not satisfy (9:1,2). There is never enough – and half-hearted tokens of God-worship are defiled by death ('bread of mourners') (9:4). Broken idols, destruction and weed-covered ruin loom (9:6). Those who continue to speak up for God are mocked (9:7,8), but there will be a reckoning (9:9).

'With their silver and gold they make idols for themselves to their own destruction. Throw out your calf-idol … a metalworker has made it; it is not God. It will be broken in pieces…'

Hosea 8:4–6

RESPOND

Take time to grieve society's rejection of God.

Bible in a year: Leviticus 23,24; Acts 12

Saturday 25 February

Hosea 9:10 – 10:15

Disappointed God

PREPARE

Do you think your behaviour has disappointed God recently? Talk with him about this.

READ

Hosea 9:10 – 10:15

EXPLORE

It was all looking so good! Grapes in the desert! God's delight in the fresh, beautiful fruit is unmistakeable (9:10a). It prompts us to think about Jesus – the true vine (John 15:1), the water of life (John 4:13,14). But...

It all went wrong when the people 'consecrated' themselves to idols. This was no casual act of getting along in the local culture, but a decisive act of commitment (9:10b). 'Planted' by God in a pleasant place, they rejected him (9:13). Their resulting wickedness brought the death of 'cherished' children, withering roots and fruitlessness (9:16) – and God would reject *them*, 'and now they must bear their guilt' (10:2).

Judgement is coming. As their fruitfulness and prosperity grew, Israel no longer acknowledged God. Arrogantly, they rejected him and their rulers. 'But even if we had a king, what could he do for us?' (10:3)! Truth was no longer dependable, and society was like a ploughed field of poisonous weeds (10:4). Hosea tells this self-satisfied country that their idols would be destroyed, its proud people enslaved, and God would punish them (10:10).

Before the final verdict, God makes a last appeal to them to seek him and reap 'the fruit of unfailing love' (10:12). But they prefer deception and dependence on their own strength... with devastating consequences (10:13–15).

> 'Sow righteousness for yourselves, reap the fruit of unfailing love ... for it is time to seek the LORD ...'
>
> **Hosea 10:12**

RESPOND

How do Hosea's words speak to your nation? To you? Seek the Lord now.

Bible in a year: Leviticus 25,26; Psalm 25

Sunday 26 February
Psalm 84

Blessed are the faithful

PREPARE

Deliberately put aside the worries and concerns of the world and of your life. Focus on God and reaffirm your trust in him as you read this psalm.

READ

Psalm 84

EXPLORE

Turn off the TV news. Put down your phone. For a few moments put your feet in the shoes of these faithful pilgrims whose goal and longing are to be in God's presence (v 2). Together with the song leaders, cry out to our living God. Let yourself be overwhelmed by his loveliness (v 2). Even the birds find welcome and protection as they make their home close to the Lord (v 3)! Today, enjoy praising God with others who also yearn 'for the living God' (v 2).

Or maybe you see yourself as a pilgrim – on your way towards God, amid difficulties and sadness. As we look to him, we find strength in our weakness ('Strengthen the feeble hands', Isaiah 35:3). God is able to transform our places of adversity (Valley of Baka, v 6) into places of abundant fruitfulness and blessing (v 6). Today, be strengthened in your faith, confident of your homecoming in God's presence (v 7).

Pause in your worship, remembering your relationship with God, and praying for your leaders (vs 8,9) whose own blessing brings peace. Turn again to your longing for God and communion with him which far surpasses anything this world may offer (v 10). Rejoice in the good things he brings to your life (v 11). Today, renew your trust in him and receive his blessing (v 12).

LORD Almighty, blessed is the one who trusts in you.

Psalm 84:12

RESPOND

Praise God!

Bible in a year: Leviticus 27; Numbers 1; Acts 13

Monday 27 February

Hosea 11:1–11

Beloved child

PREPARE

Pray for loved ones who have turned away from God.

READ

Hosea 11:1–11

EXPLORE

For a few moments, amid Hosea's damning message of judgement, it's as though we're allowed to step aside and overhear an intimate reflection of God. Here is the anguish of a loving parent (vs 1–4): 'I taught you to walk, I healed your hurts, I led you with kindness, I picked you up, I carried you, I fed you, I called you when you turned away from me...' Yet, God's children were determined to go their own way (even back to Egypt, vs 5–7). But God doesn't give up (v 8).

The Israelites' behaviour would have consequences. Refusal to repent of their idolatrous and untruthful living would result in violent defeat and bring an end to all their pretentious plans (v 6). Mere lip-service to God wasn't enough (v 7), but...

This time, surely, they'd gone too far. But how can beloved children ever be given up (v 8)? Remember the parable of Hosea's own life: 'not loved' becomes 'my loved one' (1:6; 2:1). God is more compassionate than we can imagine (vs 8,9). In response to their waywardness, he will come like a roaring lion (v 10). And then, in humility – from all directions – his people *will* return trembling, and God himself will settle them in their homes (vs 10,11). God is holy, but he loves his children.

> 'For I am God, and not a man – the Holy One among you ... he will roar like a lion. When he roars, his children will come trembling...'
>
> **Hosea 11:9,10**

RESPOND

Pray that all the nations of the world will hear God's 'roar' and turn to follow him (v 10).

Bible in a year: Numbers 2,3; Acts 14

Tuesday 28 February
Hosea 11:12 - 12:14

Look back and learn

PREPARE

Take some time to look back over your life. How has God worked through events and in your experience?

READ

Hosea 11:12 - 12:14

EXPLORE

Now Hosea reminds God's people of their past – in particular, the patriarch Jacob, and then their rescue from Egypt. Unruliness, deceit and unfaithfulness have often characterised their behaviour – and these bring consequences (11:12 – 12:2).

Jacob had been the archetypal deceiver, taking advantage of others for his own gain. In Hosea's day, untruthfulness has become the way in which society works; wealth is founded on dishonesty. Yet, those guilty do not acknowledge their sin (vs 7,8). But there is hope. God came to Jacob and 'he struggled with God'. He wept, prayed and talked with him (vs 4,5). So, Hosea tells the people, return to God. For Hosea's listeners there is a sense of possibility: wait for God (v 6).

Then, Hosea reminds the people of their rescue from Egypt (v 9). Now, looking at their idolatry and wickedness, God asks, 'Was it for *this* that I redeemed you?' (v 11).* The reference to Gilgal may recall the stones of remembrance marking their crossing of the Jordan (Joshua 4:20). Sacred memories have been desecrated. Before the words of judgement (v 14), linger over the words of verses 9 and 10. God's call to tent-living and the forgotten Festival of Tabernacles echoes the words of 2:14,15. These are words of invitation: to be with God is more important than 'bread alone'.

'... he struggled with God ... he wept and begged for his favour. He found him at Bethel and talked with him there – the LORD God Almighty, the LORD is his name!'

Hosea 12:3–5

RESPOND

Set apart time to be with God. Listen afresh to his call to you.

*Derek Kidner, *Love to the Loveless* (1981), p111

Bible in a year: Numbers 4,5; Acts 15

Wednesday 1 March

Hosea 13:1–16

I am the Lord your God...

PREPARE

'You are my Lord and my God. Amen.'

READ

Hosea 13:1–16

EXPLORE

The covenant had sealed the deal (v 4; Deuteronomy 5:1–21). God had rescued his people from Egypt, cared for them in the wilderness and led them home (vs 4–6). But they have turned against God (vs 2,9); now he will take action against them (vs 7,8). No wonder they trembled. Here, God brings charges and the sentence.

They have embraced idolatry, even the evil practices of human sacrifice (v 2). Proud and self-satisfied, they reject God's help. So much for the earthly rulers they had demanded (1 Samuel 8:19,20) – the people had got their own way, and what they deserved (vs 9–11). Now self-centred dreams 'disappear like morning mist' (v 3). And their sins are not forgotten (v 12). We can imagine God's frustration with his people who won't respond to his loving call – like 'stupid' babies at the point of birth, they haven't got the sense to be born! So, judgement will come – the east wind will blow, crops and rains will fail, storehouses will be emptied and plundered (v 15). Rebellion against God will bring unimaginable atrocities (v 16). God will have no compassion. Even those who are doing well will not be safe (v 15).

And yet, still there is a whisper of God's final triumph: 'Where, O death, is your victory?' (1 Corinthians 15:55; v 14). Judgement is not God's final word.

'I will deliver this people from the power of the grave; I will redeem them from death. Where, O death, are your plagues? Where, O grave, is your destruction?'

Hosea 13:14

RESPOND

Where do you see God's judgement at work? How might we speak his Word into troubled situations?

Bible in a year: Numbers 6,7; Psalms 26,27

Come home...

PREPARE

Turn to the Lord now: 'Forgive all our sins and receive us graciously' (Hosea 14:2).

READ

Hosea 14:1–9

EXPLORE

Now, at the end of Hosea's message – as in the parable of his marriage to Gomer (3:1–5) – our faithful God seeks out his unfaithful people speaking words of kindness and salvation. Desolate, they weren't even sure where to start, so God himself teaches them words to pray (v 2): 'Our Father, forgive us' (vs 2,3; Matthew 6:9–13). Their return begins with recognition of their sin and a rejection of false gods. Then, they can offer true worship ('the fruit of our lips', v 2). Now, they must choose to trust themselves to God's fatherly care and compassion (v 3).

With their looking to God and recognition of their hopelessness, God's response is fulsome and generous (vs 4–8). His anger is done. Forgiveness brings healing, growth and flourishing. Renewed dependence on him will bring certainty of living in his care and the knowledge that real fruitfulness is found in him alone (v 8).

So, here is Hosea's message, spoken to God's people in his time – but also, a message for today. Are we wise? Are we discerning? We also need to understand God's call to uphold his ways, to walk in obedience to him, to recognise that stumbling has its roots in his rejection – and to rejoice that we too are invited to make our home 'in his shade' (v 7).

> Who is wise? ... Who is discerning? ... The ways of the LORD are right; the righteous walk in them, but the rebellious stumble in them.
>
> **Hosea 14:9**

RESPOND

Let's check our choices, then offer ourselves to him again, to be 'a living sacrifice, holy and pleasing to God' (Romans 12:1).

Bible in a year: Numbers 8,9; Acts 16

Spotlight on...

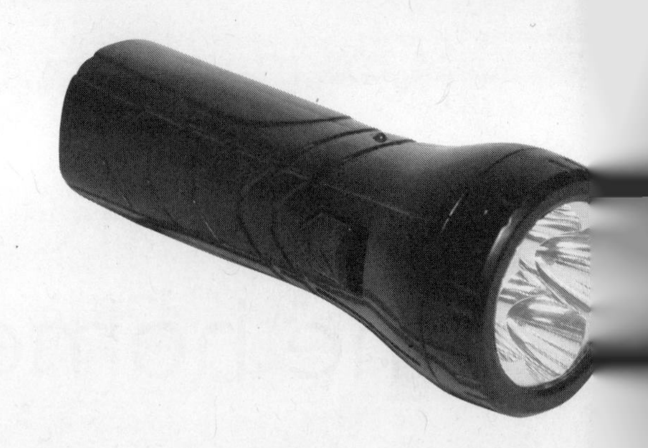

Letters

Crucial communication

Email, text messages and social media may have largely replaced letters, but the need for communication is an essential element of human existence. Over a third of the New Testament consists of letters. New churches were being established and those who founded them – the apostles and their close associates – often moved on quickly, sometimes in a matter of weeks. The Christians needed instruction, encouragement and practical advice on how to behave. Most letters are addressed to specific churches, four to individual people and others are more general. All were written to deal with issues that emerged as the church grew.

These letters are the response of the authors to the situation, written under the guidance of the Holy Spirit. They helped the early churches to understand Christian truth and to learn how God expected them to live. Thirteen are by Paul, two by Peter, one by James, one by Jude and three by John. The writer of Hebrews is unknown.

Concerned leaders

The early Christians were threatened by false teaching. Many had grown up in an immoral pagan environment and found the behaviour required of them as followers of Jesus difficult. They faced opposition from others. How would they survive, especially when those who had founded the church had moved on? In part through letters from leaders who cared.

What to believe

The letters helped the early Christians to understand God's plan for the world, human need, God's saving action in Jesus and how to respond. We discover the same truths.

How to behave

Early Christians faced many challenges and temptations as they worked out their faith in a hostile world. Some struggled with leaving behind elements of their former religious practice. Some were attracted to the more permissive moral standards of society. Our challenges may be different, but there's plenty of practical guidance for us.

Reading the letters

Remember the letters were written to people in the first century, not the twenty-first. Those were very different times, with different culture and customs.

Fill in the background

Discover all that you can about society in the first century. If the letter was written to the church in a particular location – Corinth or Philippi, for example – read about the city and ask how that might have affected the writing. If the church was founded by Paul on his missionary journeys in Acts, look at the circumstances.

Look at the content

Letters were mostly written to deal with specific issues. Think about what is going on. That may mean looking at what the letter says and asking what may have given rise to it. So, for example, Paul deals with divisions, food offered to idols and spiritual gifts in 1 Corinthians because he had received reports from the church. He writes about Jesus' return in 1 and 2 Thessalonians because he knew that they were confused. Hebrews is written to Jewish Christians under pressure to give up on Jesus and so it draws heavily on the Old Testament.

Follow the argument

The early recipients would almost certainly have heard these letters read in church in one go, not in small sections. Grasping the train of thought is easier sometimes than other times. Romans works in a logical way, while 1 Corinthians seems to move from one issue to another, and 1 John keeps returning to the twin themes of truth and love in what to modern readers may seem a rather repetitive way.

Identify the Christian truths

What does the letter say about God and the way he was working in Jesus, about the way we are put right with God, and about the work of the Holy Spirit?

Look for practical instructions

Some letters are clear and direct: the problem is not understanding but obeying. Others will not apply to us directly, and we look for the timeless principles. Eating food offered to idols, for example, is not a live issue for most of us today, but we still face temptations to compromise.

Above all, read expecting to meet God. To discover fresh truth. To be drawn to a deeper love for God. To be inspired to 'live a life worthy of the calling you have received' (Ephesians 4:1).

Writer: John Grayston

WAY IN

James 1–5

Faith in action

About the writer
Erica Roberts

Married with three adult children, Erica loves walking on a deserted beach, cold water swimming and curling up in front of a fire with a good book. She is grateful, as an Anglican Priest, for her role as City Chaplain for Older People in Southampton, and learning from the wisdom of those God has called her to serve.

I wonder how you approach the construction of flatpack furniture. Do you study the instructions meticulously, gather the appropriate tools and then research further? Or, ripping open the contents, do you assemble the pieces immediately? Most of us are probably somewhere in between. Perhaps, like me, you're happier when someone offers to tackle the project for you!

Given a similar task, I suspect James wouldn't have tolerated sitting around pondering instructions or outcomes over a cuppa, and nor would he have approved of passing the job on to someone else. He is a man of action. Passionate about his faith, James, almost certainly the half-brother of Jesus and leader of the church in Jerusalem, yearns to see others living in a way that reflects their faith and honours Jesus.

James is writing to the Messianic Jews living outside Israel, who were facing persecution and were challenged by poverty. This lively letter offers them a series of wisdom reflections, often mirroring Jesus' teaching on the Sermon on the Mount. Within this letter, there are over 50 commands, a clear sign that the focus is on action rather than theological debate.

As you read James, reflect on how you approach your own faith. Wrestling with themes of social justice and unity within the church, James calls us to action, to build that piece of flatpack furniture and not just look at the pictures! Be open to where God is prompting you to move your faith into action.

Friday 3 March
James 1:1–11

Changing focus

PREPARE

'Let us run with perseverance the race marked out for us, fixing our eyes on Jesus, the pioneer and perfecter of faith' (Hebrews 12:1,2). How has fixing your eyes on Jesus helped you during times of trial?

READ

James 1:1–11

EXPLORE

Long distance running isn't easy. It requires months of training to build physical endurance and mental determination to keep going through the pain, adverse weather and rough terrain. Perseverance, James tells us, builds character, and brings us to maturity (v 4).

James grabs our attention by challenging us to consider it pure joy to face trials in our lives (v 2). Why? Because through the experience of hardship and struggle our faith can grow and mature. Learning to trust God in all circumstances builds perseverance, a quality that was perfectly ascribed to Jesus who 'For the joy that was set before him he endured the cross' (Hebrews 12:2).

Our faith can seem like a long-distance run. It can be exhilarating, but just as the runner develops perseverance for those long, painful and lonely stretches, so through times of suffering we develop confidence in a faithful God. Like a young child who has learned absolute trust in his or her parents, we can ask for all we need when times get tough, knowing that God will never abandon us. This changes our focus on life. Trials may not be welcome, but we can *choose* to approach hardship with hope, in the knowledge that through them God will change us.

Consider it pure joy, my brothers and sisters, whenever you face trials of many kinds.

James 1:2

RESPOND

Are we ready to change our focus, choosing to trust God in all circumstances for this long-distance journey of faith?

Bible in a year: Numbers 10,11; Acts 17

Saturday 4 March

James 1:12–18

Entangled in a spiderweb

PREPARE

We all are vulnerable to temptation. Reflect honestly on your own struggles, asking God, who gives us every good and perfect gift (v 17), to provide us with the grace and strength to resist temptation in our own lives.

READ

James 1:12–18

EXPLORE

Temptation is like being caught in a spiderweb. The beauty of the web entices us to look closer and yet once we've taken that first step, as James so vividly portrays, we become trapped. We are unable to pull back, where desire leads to sin, and we become entangled in a web that eventually leads to death (v 15). How easy it is to take that first step: just one drink, just one white lie, just one quick look… Of course, the list is endless.

However, temptation does not come from God (vs 13,14). We can be misled into thinking that our personal desires will bring life, but Jesus reminds us that Satan only comes 'to steal and kill and destroy' (John 10:10). God's amazing gift is the crown of life for all those who persevere (v 12). It's repeated in Revelation 2:10: 'Be faithful, even to the point of death, and I will give you life as your victor's crown.' This gift of everlasting honour and praise is bestowed on all those who endure trials and temptations, living faithfully for Christ.

> Blessed is the one who perseveres under trial because, having stood the test, that person will receive the crown of life that the Lord has promised to those who love him.
>
> **James 1:12**

RESPOND

Seek God's forgiveness for those times when temptation trips us up. Receive the blessing of God's good gift for us, the crown of life and new birth through the word of truth (v 18), our Lord Jesus Christ.

Bible in a year: Numbers 12–14; Psalms 28,29

Sunday 5 March
Psalm 85

God's promise of restoration

PREPARE

Where have you seen God's steadfast love bring restoration in the life of your church? Give thanks as you recall God's faithfulness.

READ

Psalm 85

EXPLORE

Reading this psalm, I wonder how the words resonate with the health of your own church communities. God has liberated the people of Israel from exile (vs 1–3) and yet they were still unsure of God's favour, struggling to rebuild their place of worship and their livelihoods. How could they be confident of God's love and faithfulness?

With increasing secularisation and declining church membership across the UK, we are also a faith community in crisis. The generational decline is particularly disturbing. Current statistics indicate 70 per cent of under-30s identifying as non-religious, with only half of young people from Christian homes retaining their parents' faith. Despite this our churches remain at the heart of our communities, caring for the poor, providing sanctuary for the homeless and friendship for the lonely.

Like Israel, we cry out in prayer for restoration and revival for God's church (v 6). We yearn to have communities raising their voices in praise as men and women, young and old, turn back to Jesus. Let's be encouraged by God's promises illustrated so beautifully by the psalmist (vs 8–13). Research suggests that intergenerational friendship, listening to the global concerns of the young, wrestling together with faith issues and recognising the prophetic voice of this generation,* will ensure that our churches remain relevant, living out the radically transforming shalom of Jesus.

> Will you not revive us again, that your people may rejoice in you?
>
> **Psalm 85:6**

RESPOND

How can we affirm the prophetic voice of the younger generation?

*www.churchtimes.co.uk/articles/2020/31-january/features/features/how-faith-survives-the-turbulent-twenties

Bible in a year: Numbers 15,16; Acts 18

Monday 6 March

James 1:19–27

The implanted Word

PREPARE

Give thanks for the wisdom, truth and saving grace of God's Word. Consider what helps you go deeper in your relationship with God and nurtures your faith.

READ

James 1:19–27

EXPLORE

Gardeners know the importance of planting seeds in fertile soil, and nurturing their growth with water, nutrients and the occasional weeding! This takes time, care and painstaking research. For God's implanted Word (v 21) to germinate and become fruitful in our own lives, we need to provide fertile soil, by rejecting all that causes harm to ourselves and others, so we can be fully open to all that God's Word can teach us.

James gives us practical advice to aid the fruitfulness of God's Word in our lives: to listen, to speak only after careful consideration and be slow to anger (v 19). This is a huge challenge for some of us, and yet is essential advice that enables our relationships to flourish.

But listening is not enough. Our passage compares listening and not acting on God's Word with looking at ourselves in a mirror and then forgetting what we have seen (vs 23–25). If we look deeply into God's Word, our response is not to live without reference to this freedom, but to step out in obedience, acting on all that God's living Word offers. Implanted with God's Word, we are challenged to grow in practical holiness and to share God's compassion for those who are in most need in our churches and community (v 27).

Do not merely listen to the word, and so deceive yourselves. Do what it says.

James 1:22

RESPOND

How can we become 'doers and not just hearers' of God's Word today?

Bible in a year: Numbers 17–19; Acts 19

Tuesday 7 March
James 2:1–13

No favouritism

PREPARE

'You are precious and honoured in my sight, and ... I love you' (Isaiah 43:4a). As you reflect on God's love for you, how does this help you respond to the challenge to 'love your neighbour as yourself' (v 8)?

READ

James 2:1–13

EXPLORE

Recognising the danger of personal discrimination, many job applications are required to be anonymised, with no reference to gender, age or ethnicity. Partiality creeps into our lives and our common human tendency is to defer to those most likely to benefit us.

However, this is not God's way. 'People look at the outward appearance, but the Lord looks at the heart' (1 Samuel 16:7b). If we believe in the glory of Jesus (v 1), then we are called to reflect this truth. James illustrates partiality through the favour shown to someone with wealth and influence, a theme not unfamiliar in our churches today (vs 2,3). Building on this illustration, James emphasises that spiritual riches are not related to material wealth, and by rejecting the poor, the vulnerable and those different from ourselves, we place ourselves as judge, rejecting God's sovereignty (v 7).

In obeying God's royal law (v 8), our faith becomes characterised by action, not just words (v 12), seeking to value everyone as equal. James concludes with the good news that God will judge with mercy (v 13), when we have also treated others with compassion and love.

If you really keep the royal law found in Scripture, 'Love your neighbour as yourself,' you are doing right.

James 2:8

RESPOND

Ask for God's grace to become more open-hearted and welcoming to those you find difficult to treat as an equal.

Bible in a year: Numbers 20,21; Acts 20

Wednesday 8 March

James 2:14–26

Can such faith save you?

PREPARE

Rejoice in this truth: 'For it is by grace you have been saved, through faith – and this is not from yourselves, it is the gift of God' (Ephesians 2:8).

READ

James 2:14–26

EXPLORE

I wonder how your faith affects the world around you. It can be easy to participate in church activities, commend sermons, engage in Bible studies and enjoy worshipping together – and yet not live out this faith in our daily context. James, although provocatively asking, 'Can such faith save you?' (v 14), is practically challenging us to understand what difference it makes to believe in a generous and compassionate God. Surely, the heart of our faith is to live in this light, responding with love and practical care for the poor and oppressed (vs 16,17).

James is not suggesting that faith is dependent on our actions, but rather that the natural response to a living faith is through our actions. For example, Abraham's longstanding faith in the promises of God preceded his obedience to a bewildering command (v 21). In stark contrast, Rahab, a prostitute, proclaiming God as Lord of heaven and earth (Joshua 2:11), risks her life for others (v 25).

Whoever we are, whatever our background, true faith is expressed through our desire to consecrate our lives fully to a faithful God and to all those he loves. James is calling us to action, to be Jesus' representatives in our churches, communities and wider world.

> What good is it, my brothers and sisters, if someone claims to have faith but has no deeds? Can such faith save them?
>
> **James 2:14**

RESPOND

Mother Teresa said: 'Faith in action is love, and love in action is service.' How can you put your faith into action today?

Bible in a year: Numbers 22,23; Psalm 30

Thursday 9 March

James 3:1–12

The power of the tongue

PREPARE

'Praise the Lord. How good it is to sing praises to our God, how pleasant and fitting to praise him!' (Psalm 147:1).

READ

James 3:1–12

EXPLORE

With eight intertwining muscles and over 2,000 taste buds, the tongue is the only muscle working independently from our skeleton. Its appearance provides clues about our health. As James clearly elucidates, our tongue also reflects our spiritual health, being a force for good or evil.

I wonder how often you regret something you've said and wish you could retract a comment or email or gossip from the coffee room. Perhaps you've been the recipient of harmful innuendo or backstabbing stories, or been tempted through the impure speech of another.

The tongue is powerful. Metaphors of a horse's bit (v 3) or a ship's rudder (v 4) illustrate how one small mistake with our tongue can change the direction of another's life. Whereas we have initial control over what we say, once it's left our mouth, the damage becomes uncontrollable, like a forest fire set alight from a tiny spark (vs 5,6).

What comes from our mouth reflects our inner life, the place where we seek to nurture holy lives in the image of Christ. Yet it's easy to bless others in one moment, then cause untold harm in the next (vs 9,10). We all make mistakes (v 2), but let's take the rudder and hold firm against worldly winds and steer the course of blessing and praise.

Out of the same mouth come praise and cursing. My brothers and sisters, this should not be.

James 3:10

RESPOND

'Train' your tongue by raising your voice to praise God or read a favourite scripture out loud.

Bible in a year: Numbers 24,25; Acts 21

Friday 10 March

James 3:13–18

Growing in wisdom

PREPARE

Give thanks for the wisdom you have received from others. Reflect on what it was about the lives of these people that enabled them to offer you wisdom.

READ

James 3:13–18

EXPLORE

Not surprisingly, research suggests that wisdom doesn't always grow with age (see Job's question, 12:12), nor is it related to intelligence. Rather, wisdom is associated with inherent character traits, which pursue moral virtue and emotional self-control.

Charles Spurgeon, a famous nineteenth-century preacher, explained it like this: 'Wisdom is the right use of knowledge. To know is not to be wise. Many men know a great deal and are all the greater fools for it. There is no fool so great a fool as a knowing fool. But to know how to use knowledge is to have wisdom.'*

Our desire as disciples of Jesus is to pursue wisdom that enables us to view life from God's perspective, wisdom reflected in the virtues described by James (v 17), fruit borne only by walking closely with God. Proverbs reminds us that 'the fear of the LORD is the beginning of wisdom' (9:10). The way of wisdom begins with our reverence and knowledge of God, a knowledge that shapes our lives as we seek to reflect the Lord's glory, being transformed into his likeness (see 2 Corinthians 3:18). This is true wisdom and wisdom that can indeed grow with age if we prayerfully prioritise our relationship with Jesus.

> ... the wisdom that comes from heaven is first of all pure; then peace-loving, considerate, submissive, full of mercy and good fruit, impartial and sincere.
>
> **James 3:17**

RESPOND

Ask for God's gift of wisdom, so that you can lead a holy, peaceful and gentle life.

*Charles H Spurgeon, *Metropolitan Tabernacle Pulpit*, Volume 17

Bible in a year: Numbers 26,27; Acts 22

Saturday 11 March
James 4:1–12

Joining the defence line

PREPARE

Sit quietly as you pray: 'Lord Jesus Christ, have mercy on me, a sinner.' Open your hands to receive the Holy Spirit afresh today.

READ

James 4:1–12

EXPLORE

This is a tough passage and as usual James doesn't mince his words. Speaking of war (v 1) and adultery (v 4) as metaphors for the state of our Christian communities is *meant* to be uncomfortable. Sadly, we have all experienced discord, hostility and self-seeking behaviour within our churches. The source of this strife comes from our internal battle zones as we wrestle with the temptation of worldly pleasures. How easy it is to put our own desires before those of God.

Peter warns that the devil is like a prowling lion waiting patiently for his prey, moving quietly and unseen (1 Peter 5:8). Similarly, we need to be alert and on guard to ward off the devil (v 7), who, like the lion, targets our weaknesses and vulnerabilities.

Both war and adultery leave devastation in their wake. James paints a picture of spiritual adultery destroying our relationship with God (v 4). The only remedy is to submit ourselves to God (v 7). This doesn't mean sitting back and doing nothing, but instead intentionally joining the defence line in the battlefield. How amazing that God is jealous for his Spirit within us (v 5), and when we draw close to him in active submission, God promises us the grace to resist the devil and all temptation.

Submit yourselves, then, to God. Resist the devil, and he will flee from you.

James 4:7

RESPOND

Pray for unity within your own church family, asking the Holy Spirit to intervene where there is discord or hostility.

Bible in a year: Numbers 28,29; Psalm 31

Sunday 12 March

Psalm 86

Walking in God's way

PREPARE

Read Psalm 86 slowly and prayerfully. Ask God to highlight a phrase that speaks to you. Repeat the phrase, inviting the Holy Spirit to teach you more about the truth of God's Word for your own life.

READ

Psalm 86

EXPLORE

We recently celebrated the arrival of our first grandchild. What a miracle watching this small baby acquire new skills as he grows and develops. Over time he will learn by mirroring those around him, as his parents teach and encourage him at each new stage. The character of this small boy will, in no small part, be a result of being taught well by those who love and invest in him (v 16).

The same applies as we seek to grow in spiritual maturity. Despite the psalmist crying out at a time of great need, he recognises the necessity of being taught God's ways, learning to depend more whole-heartedly on God. Declaring God's sovereignty (v 9), the psalmist yearns to approach God with an undivided heart (v 11). An undivided heart is a humble heart, a heart aware that there is always more to learn about God's character and a heart that grows to depend on God more fully.

How easy it is for our circumstances to distract us from following God's way, from depending on God in times of need (vs 6,7). Yet, God's desire is to teach us his way of truth and for us to mirror his character with an undivided heart.

Teach me your way, LORD, that I may rely on your faithfulness; give me an undivided heart, that I may fear your name.

Psalm 86:11

RESPOND

Praise God for the amazing promise that Jesus is the way, the truth and the life (John 14:6).

Bible in a year: Numbers 30,31; Acts 23

Monday 13 March

James 4:13–17

What is your life?

PREPARE

Giving thanks for your life, reflect on its brevity within the eternal timeframe. 'The life of mortals ... they flourish like a flower of the field; the wind blows over it and it is gone...' (Psalm 103:15,16).

READ

James 4:13–17

EXPLORE

I love planning – sorting through my work diary, looking ahead as I organise holidays and family gatherings. But I'm challenged by the opening of this passage, addressed originally to wealthy merchants across Palestine and the Mediterranean, as they confidently declare plans for their trading activities (v 13). There is an arrogance in presuming that self-sufficient planning brings success.

Not that planning is wrong, but planning without including God is not only foolish, but is named as sinful (v 17). Thinking back to livelihoods devastated by the Covid-19 pandemic emphasises the fragility of our existence and the importance of trusting in God for our future and not relying on our own insights (Proverbs 3:5).

Life is precious, a gift from God – and only he knows the number of our days. Our response should be one of prayerful obedience, listening to God for our future, being prepared to change direction if necessary, and holding all our plans lightly. Planning can be good stewardship, but only if we place our dependence on God and embrace his sovereign purpose in our lives (v 15).

Why, you do not even know what will happen tomorrow. What is your life? You are a mist that appears for a little while and then vanishes.

James 4:14

RESPOND

Despite the transitory nature of our earthly lives, rejoice that the steadfast love of the Lord is 'from everlasting to everlasting' on 'those who fear him' (Psalm 103:17).

Bible in a year: Numbers 32,33; Acts 24

Tuesday 14 March

James 5:1–12

Living with integrity

PREPARE

I wonder how challenging you find it to tell the truth in every situation. Ask God to guard your heart so you can grow in honesty and integrity.

READ

James 5:1–12

EXPLORE

As a nation we have become increasingly cynical about the honesty of our politicians, suspicious about the motives of large corporations, and even dubious about those we rely on daily for health, financial and household support. Who can we trust? It sometimes feels as though our lives are governed by those described as living 'on earth in luxury and self-indulgence' (v 5), without regard for the common good of society.

Living with integrity begins by being truthful in all areas of our lives and letting our 'Yes' be yes and our 'No' be no (v 12). Truth and trust are intimately connected. We learn to trust those who we know are telling us the truth. James goes further to emphasise the importance of truth-telling, by warning against using oaths, or invoking the name of God. In *all* of our words we should seek to be truthful and, therefore, trustworthy.

Oaths are not prohibited in Scripture (eg Numbers 30:2), but James was writing to Jews who were abusing God's name and not following through on their promises, thus defaming the name and character of God. The important message here is truthful communication, providing building blocks for healthy relationships. This means walking honestly with God, in humility and vulnerability, so others will see God's truth reflected in our lives.

> ... do not swear – not by heaven, or by earth or by anything else. All you need to say is a simple 'Yes' or 'No'. Otherwise you will be condemned.
>
> **James 5:12**

RESPOND

Praise Jesus that he is the Truth (John 14:6; 17:17).

Bible in a year: Numbers 34,35; Acts 25

Wednesday 15 March

James 5:13–20

Prayer untapped

PREPARE

Begin by reflecting on how you pray. What do you find helpful? What hinders you praying? How could you refresh the rhythms of your prayer life?

READ

James 5:13–20

EXPLORE

James brings us full circle as he concludes his letter. Asking God for wisdom began this missive (1:5) and now, after extensive advice on how to practically live out our faith, James concludes by reminding us of the importance of prayer. In the film *Shadowlands*, CS Lewis reflected that, 'It doesn't change God; it changes me.' Without drawing on this untapped resource, without depending on the power of God, our desire to resist temptation, to live generously and grow in wisdom will inevitably fail.

Prayer acknowledges our fragility and an intimacy with God that reaches out in our suffering and rejoices with him in our gladness (v 13). It can feel safer to pray alone, and yet being prayed for by our leaders (v 14), praying with others and confessing our sins together (v 16) recognise that we are part of a community of faith, caring for each other, believing that prayer is 'powerful and effective' (v 16).

Being reminded of Elijah, who patiently persevered in prayer (vs 17,18),* encourages us that sharing our own stories of prayer strengthens our faith and deepens our dependence on God. Together, let's make prayer a habit, one that reaches out to an immutable, dependable, powerful God – a habit which transforms us and our communities.

The prayer of a righteous person is powerful and effective.

James 5:16b

RESPOND

'Rejoice always, pray continually, give thanks in all circumstances…' (1 Thessalonians 5:16–18).

*1 Kings 17:1; 18:43–45

Bible in a year: Numbers 36; Deuteronomy 1; Psalm 32

A wideness in God's mercy

For a small book, Jonah packs a big punch. For a minor prophet, Jonah has some major truths to teach, not least about the immensity of God's love, mercy and grace.

It is easy when reading Jonah to get sidetracked about whether it is true. Was Jonah really swallowed by a great fish? Personally, I take the book at face value.

To get bogged down in such questions is to miss the main point. This charming story is really about the character of God, and the scandal of grace.

There is within each of us a tendency to think our culture is the best, and that our nation is particularly favoured by God. Such pride is always likely to limit our appreciation of God's great love. Most of us, like Jonah, need to push back our boundaries and remember that his love reaches *all* people, everywhere. God has no favourites.

Jonah gained notoriety as the runaway prophet – but why did he run away? What did he fear might happen if he preached to Nineveh? Did he suspect the merciful God might actually be kind to that wicked city? Was he unnerved, not by the possibility of judgement, but by the possibility of God showing mercy and forgiving them?

Let's see what the story has to say.

About the writer
Tony Horsfall

After graduating from London School of Theology, Tony served as a missionary in East Malaysia, then as a pastor in West Yorkshire. Since 2004 he has had his own ministry, Charis Training. He is a retreat leader, author and mentor.

Thursday 16 March

Jonah 1:1–16

The narrow-minded prophet

PREPARE

Ask that God will speak to you as we begin these readings in the book of Jonah and reveal any prejudices you may have in the light of his amazing love.

READ

Jonah 1:1–16

EXPLORE

I ran away from home once. I had done something wrong, and expected to be in trouble, so I ran into the fields behind our house and hid among the trees. Happily, my mother came and found me. I said sorry and that was the end of the matter.

Jonah ran away to Tarshish not because he had done something bad, but because he suspected God wanted to do something good. Nineveh was a violent city, the capital of a barbaric superpower called Assyria. At first, he was perhaps pleased that God wanted to confront these wicked foreigners with their crimes and give them their just deserts. But then (according to his own words in 4:2) a troubling thought seized him. What if Nineveh responded to his preaching and repented? God would be obliged to forgive them, and Jonah couldn't stomach the thought of that.

Grace is good when we are the recipients, but can seem troublesome when others are beneficiaries, especially those who don't deserve it. Our inbuilt prejudices and warped sense of fair play can make us narrow-minded, cutting us off from the heart of God, which as the hymnwriter says 'is most wonderfully kind' (FW Faber, 1814–63).

> The word of the LORD came to Jonah ... 'Go to the great city of Nineveh and preach against it, because its wickedness has come up before me.'
>
> **Jonah 1:1,2**

RESPOND

Have you ever been tempted to turn your back on God? What happened? How does the mercy of God give us hope at such times?

Bible in a year: Deuteronomy 2,3; Acts 26

Friday 17 March

Jonah 1:17 – 2:10

A time to rethink

PREPARE

Sit quietly for a moment and seek to relax. Breathe slowly and deeply. Hand your cares over to the God who loves you and watches over you, even in your distress.

READ

Jonah 1:17 – 2:10

EXPLORE

I have occasionally invited retreat groups to use their imagination to enter into a Bible story. I'm not sure this part of Jonah's story would be suitable though. Not everyone could cope with the graphic imagery it might suggest!

It is instructive to see how God engineered circumstances to bring the reluctant prophet to a place where he could face up to his own inner reality, first through the storm (1:4) and then through the huge fish (1:17). There in the darkness of the belly of the fish Jonah is alone, confronted by God and his own hardness of heart.

Jonah was there for three days and nights. It seems to suggest a resurrection-type experience where he is called to die to his own will and ways, and let go of his prejudices (2:7–9). Only then can he come forth from the darkness into the light of a new day and a second chance (2:10).

The mercy of God is not just for wicked Ninevites, but also reaches disobedient and stubborn prophets. It means there is always a way back and a chance to recalibrate our hearts.

'In my distress I called to the LORD, and he answered me. From deep in the realm of the dead I called for help, and you listened to my cry.'

Jonah 2:2

RESPOND

Think back over your life to any time of enforced stillness. What happened to make you slow down? What did you learn, if anything, from the experience?

Bible in a year: Deuteronomy 4,5; Acts 27

Saturday 18 March

Jonah 3:1–10

Mercy overflowing

PREPARE

We are able to come boldly before God because Jesus has opened up for us a new and living way (Hebrews 10:20). Draw near today, however you may feel.

READ

Jonah 3:1–10

EXPLORE

It is a chastened Jonah who arrives on the outskirts of the great city of Nineveh. Nervously he passes through the city gates and proclaims: 'Forty more days and Nineveh will be overthrown' (3:4). Not exactly a message guaranteed to increase his popularity, yet he faithfully delivers the word God has given him.

Then, the first surprise. King and people repent of their wickedness with a genuine show of contrition (vs 5–9). Then the second surprise. God sees their genuine sorrow and how they turn from their evil ways, and in his mercy turns from his anger and forgives them.

Jonah is angry because it seems so unfair that after all their wickedness the Ninevites should be forgiven. He is now obedient, but his heart is still lagging behind. He is confounded by the generosity of God, confused by the mercy shown to such undeserving people. This is the scandal of grace. It contradicts human ideas of justice.

Jonah reminds me of the elder brother in the story of the prodigal son (Luke 15:11–32). He too was affronted by the father's generous love. Grace is always so totally undeserved.

'Let everyone call urgently on God. Let them give up their evil ways ... Who knows? God may yet relent and with compassion turn from his fierce anger so that we will not perish.'

Jonah 3:8,9

RESPOND

Does it upset you that people who have done truly wicked deeds might be forgiven? How might the story of Jonah help you with this?

Bible in a year: Deuteronomy 6,7; Psalm 33

Glorious things

PREPARE

Thank God today for the opportunity to worship together with other people. Ask that your hearts will be filled with a spirit of praise as you meet together.

READ

Psalm 87

EXPLORE

This psalm is the basis for a well-known hymn by John Newton (1725–1807), which begins 'Glorious things of thee are spoken, Zion city of our God'. Like the psalm, it celebrates the joy of being one of the people of God, and the grace that has given us such a favoured position.

Zion was the hill on which Jerusalem was built, and it came to be known as the city of God. The psalmist considers it a great privilege to have been born there. Throughout Scripture Zion came to represent the church, and so this psalm speaks to us of the privilege that we have when we are born again and included in the family of God, with our names written in heaven (Hebrews 12:22–24).

For those of us who know God in this way, worship is a natural response to such grace. Music and singing are instinctive responses to the goodness of God and rightly characterise our worship. We find our strength and joy in God. The Spirit within us becomes a spring of water bubbling up, or a fountain overflowing with life (John 4:14; 7:38).

As they make music they will sing, 'All my fountains are in you.'

Psalm 87:7

RESPOND

Ponder the privilege of being a child of God, and the miracle of the new birth. How good it is to belong to the people of God!

Bible in a year: Deuteronomy 8,9; Acts 28

Monday 20 March

Jonah 4:1–11

The heart of God

PREPARE

Take a moment to consider the character of God, especially his extraordinary love. Remind yourself that you are the object of that love, and the Father takes delight in you, his child.

READ

Jonah 4:1–11

EXPLORE

Poor Jonah falls into a deep depression after what happened in Nineveh, convinced that God had made a mistake. He feels he wants to die (vs 3,8,9), but God deals with him very tenderly, helping him understand his heart of love, and why he cares for the Ninevites.

Notice again how God orchestrates events with the leafy plant (v 6), a very hungry worm (v 7) and then a scorching east wind (v 8) – all expressions of the providence of God and designed to speak to Jonah. The punchline comes right at the end of the story. If Jonah can show compassion towards a plant, how much more should God have compassion on the people and animals in Nineveh?

The book of Jonah is like a missionary tract written to encourage the people of Israel to reach out with God's love to the surrounding nations. It speaks to us of the largeness of the heart of God and his compassion for those who do not know him. This burden is something that he wants to form in us as well, lifting us out of our comfort and complacency to respond to the needs of the world.

'I knew that you are a gracious and compassionate God, slow to anger and abounding in love, a God who relents from sending calamity.'

Jonah 4:2

RESPOND

'Lord, forgive me when I am absorbed in my own concerns and fail to see the needs around me. Give me your heart of compassion and a will to obey you.'

Bible in a year: Deuteronomy 10,11; Romans 1

Before I leave you

About the writer
Jennie Pollock

Jennie is Head of Public Policy at the Christian Medical Fellowship, and a writer and editor. Her first book, on contentment, is available now. She lives, works and worships in central London, blogs at jenniepollock.com and tweets as @missjenniep

Jesus' triumphal entry into Jerusalem marked the beginning of the final week before his arrest and crucifixion. As we read through these chapters, it becomes clear that Jesus knows his time is coming to an end and wants to make sure he says everything he needs to. He starts to make more provocative statements to the religious leaders. He spends a lot of time in the Temple courts, teaching and preaching the gospel. And he gives his followers hints about the persecutions to come, along with instructions about how to face them.

But first, we will see him demonstrating exactly what kind of king he is: the kind that comes humbly, riding the foal of a donkey.

We will get an insight into his heart, too, which will help set the context for some of the harsh things he says to the scribes, Pharisees and teachers of the law: he weeps over Jerusalem.

For hundreds of years this city, with its glorious Temple in the centre, had been the place on earth where God's presence was most tangibly manifested. Yet when the Son of the King came to it, this royal city would completely fail to recognise him. Or perhaps, as we will see in the parable of the vineyard, those who should have been most eagerly awaiting him *would* recognise him and would knowingly turn against him.

No wonder he wept.

Tuesday 21 March

Luke 19:28–44

The king on a colt

PREPARE

Sometimes the Scriptures become so familiar they lose their wonder and impact. As you read today's passage, try to imagine what the different characters were thinking and feeling. How might you have reacted if you'd been there?

READ

Luke 19:28–44

EXPLORE

In two of the other Gospel accounts of this episode (Matthew 21:1–9; John 12:12–15), we are told that Jesus' decision to ride a colt into Jerusalem was the fulfilment of a prophecy in Zechariah 9:9. The long-awaited saviour and true King of Israel would come to his people riding on the foal of a donkey.

All other conquering kings in history, and in myths and legends, have come to claim their throne riding on impressive, powerful beasts, not on untrained baby donkeys! Jesus' mode of transport was yet another hint to his followers that his kingdom and reign would be very different from anything the world had ever seen. They would be marked by humility, not by great pomp and circumstance.

Jesus knew that neither the crowds shouting their praises nor the Pharisees who rebuked them had really understood what was going on (vs 38–40). As he caught sight of Jerusalem, he wept (v 41), knowing that its people would not embrace their salvation but would turn away from it, leading to their destruction. Jerusalem was besieged and destroyed, as Jesus prophesied, in AD 70 (vs 43,44).

'Go to the village ahead of you, and as you enter it, you will find a colt tied there, which no one has ever ridden. Untie it and bring it here.'

Luke 19:30

RESPOND

Jesus weeps over all those who reject him, not wanting anyone to be lost (2 Peter 3:9). Ask him for his heart of compassion for those who do not yet know him.

Bible in a year: Deuteronomy 12–14; Romans 2

Wednesday 22 March
Luke 19:45 - 20:8

Right question, wrong motive

PREPARE

The seat of prayer and worship is no longer the Temple in Jerusalem, but is now in our hearts. Clear aside the clutter and pray as you come to God's Word.

READ

Luke 19:45 - 20:8

EXPLORE

When a new teacher comes along performing miracles and teaching new things, it is right for leaders in the church to question his credentials. They have a duty to protect their 'flock' from being led astray. These leaders were asking the right questions, but with a very wrong motive.

In Acts we read that the Berean Jews were praised for being of 'noble character' when Paul went and preached the gospel to them. They didn't just blindly accept or reject it, but 'they received the message with great eagerness and examined the Scriptures every day to see if what Paul said was true' (Acts 17:11).

These chief priests and teachers of the law should equally have been eagerly looking for the Messiah. When someone came along doing Messiah-like things and bringing new teaching, they should have searched the Scriptures with eyes of hope to see whether what he was saying and doing was in line with God's Word.

Jesus knew that these priests and teachers weren't seeking truth or trying to protect the people from false teaching. They were simply trying to preserve their own position.

'Tell us by what authority you are doing these things,' they said. 'Who gave you this authority?'
Luke 20:2

RESPOND

Like the Pharisees, we can easily become hard-hearted to anything that challenges our thinking or lifestyle – or accept unbiblical teaching because it makes us feel good. Ask the Lord to show you any areas where you are resisting his Word.

Bible in a year: Deuteronomy 15,16; Psalm 34

Thursday 23 March

Luke 20:9–19

An invitation to repentance

PREPARE

God sent his beloved Son to us, knowing all we would do to him. Thank him for stopping at nothing to save you from destruction.

READ

Luke 20:9–19

EXPLORE

In the Old Testament, the grapevine is often used as an image for Israel, the people of God. So when Jesus told this parable, he wasn't just picking a type of agriculture at random; he was very deliberately speaking against those who had been left in charge of God's people.

The 'tenant farmers' in the story represent the priests and teachers of the law. I picture them standing at a distance, listening in as Jesus taught the people. They would certainly have understood Jesus' meaning. How do you think they felt? How would you feel, being openly criticised in front of people who looked up to you?

But Jesus never spoke out about people just to shame them. He never wants to condemn, but rather to convict. Condemnation leaves us in our sin; conviction is an invitation to repent and receive God's forgiveness. Sadly, verse 19 shows that the chief priests and teachers had closed their hearts to this Son whom God loved. They loved the good things their role brought them more than doing what was right. When the Son came, they chose to destroy him, not worship him.

'Then the owner of the vineyard said, "What shall I do? I will send my son, whom I love; perhaps they will respect him."'

Luke 20:13

RESPOND

How do you respond when God points out areas of sin in your life? Do you put up your barriers and try to ignore him? Or do you welcome his invitation to turn back to him and receive his love and forgiveness once again?

Bible in a year: Deuteronomy 17,18; Romans 3

Friday 24 March
Luke 20:20–26

To give him his due

PREPARE

Of all the things you have to do today, all the people you have to help and serve and please, there is One who, above all, deserves your attention. Give it to him now as you come to his Word.

READ

Luke 20:20–26

EXPLORE

How many images of people have you seen in the past 24 hours? Photos of family and friends, pictures in magazines and newspapers, moving images on the TV... We are so surrounded by representations of people's faces, we no longer pay much attention. In Jesus' time, none of those things existed. The only place most people would ever have seen the image of another person was on coins.

Imprinting Caesar's face on those pieces of metal was a way of marking his ownership. Similarly, God has imprinted his own image on each of us, showing to all of creation that we are his.

Paying taxes to a ruler is an expression of allegiance to him. It acknowledges his rule and reign, and gives him some recompense for the infrastructure and protection he provides. We humans bear the image of our Ruler (Genesis 1:26), so how should we express our allegiance to him? How can we use our lives to acknowledge his sovereignty and give him some small recompense for his infinite provision and protection?

He said to them, 'Then give back to Caesar what is Caesar's, and to God what is God's.'

Luke 20:25

RESPOND

'Father God, you have made us and stamped your image on us. Thank you for the honour of bearing your image in the sight of all creation. Help us to live in ways that honour you and point others towards you. Amen.'

Bible in a year: Deuteronomy 19,20; Romans 4

Saturday 25 March

Luke 20:27–44

What happens when we die?

PREPARE

'I saw the LORD, high and exalted, seated on a throne; and the train of his robe filled the temple' (Isaiah 6:1). Use this picture today, to help you focus on God's great glory.

READ

Luke 20:27–44

EXPLORE

Understanding what happens when we die is one of mankind's enduring questions. This passage doesn't answer it fully, but it should fill us with hope.

Jesus showed the Sadducees that their thinking on this was too small. Heaven will not simply be an extension of this life, with its loss, loneliness and lusts. We won't need to produce children to continue our species. We won't need the companionship of one 'special' person to keep us happy. And we will have pleasures far greater than sexual intercourse can offer. The apostle Paul tells us that marriage is given to us, at least in part, as a picture of the relationship between Christ and the Church – the worldwide body of believers (Ephesians 5:32). We will neither want nor need another union when that one is complete.

All believers should remember that union with Christ is the ultimate goal – not marriage or any of the other good things we enjoy on earth – and must live with that in mind.

'He is not the God of the dead, but of the living, for to him all are alive.'

Luke 20:38

RESPOND

'Lord, please help me recognise when I am getting caught up in worldly cares. Show me what it means to live in the light of my eternal future life with you. Amen.'

Bible in a year: Deuteronomy 21,22; Psalm 35

Sunday 26 March

Psalm 88

Faith in the darkness

PREPARE

What is your mood like today? Tell God how you are feeling – about life, about the things ahead of you, and about spending time with him. Don't be afraid to be honest (he already knows).

READ

Psalm 88

EXPLORE

For many believers, times of deep despair and depression can be a persistent part of life. The psalmist here is clearly in a dark season and has experienced suffering and sorrow since his youth (v 15). His struggles surround him, his friends have abandoned him and even God feels distant.

Yet look at his faith, even in the midst of this torment: although his trust in God is deeply shaken, still it is to God he turns. He knows God is the only person who can save him (v 1). And he knows God is in control. He says, '*You* have put me in the lowest pit ... *you* have overwhelmed me' (vs 6,7, emphasis added).

He also appeals to God's glory (vs 10–12). This is a similar appeal to the ones Moses makes in Exodus 32:11–14 and 33:15,16 – God's reputation is at stake. If for no other reason, he should save his people so they can witness to his goodness.

It is not sinful to feel sad or despairing. This psalm reminds us that in our darkest moments we can still speak honestly to God and call on him to help us.

> LORD, you are the God who saves me; day and night I cry out to you.
>
> **Psalm 88:1**

RESPOND

If you are feeling low or suffering, write an honest prayer expressing how you feel. Pray for those you know who are suffering, particularly those prone to depression.

Bible in a year: Deuteronomy 23,24; Romans 5

Monday 27 March

Luke 20:45 – 21:4

Giving him our all

PREPARE

'All to Jesus I surrender / All to him I freely give; / I will ever love and trust him, / In his presence daily live.'* Say or sing these words with your hands open to symbolise surrender.

READ

Luke 20:45 – 21:4

EXPLORE

Have you ever been with someone who makes controversial statements embarrassingly loudly? I wonder whether Jesus was doing that here. Was he speaking loudly enough for the passing teachers of the law to hear his criticism of their prideful strutting, or for the poor widow to hear his praise? We have no way of knowing, but it seems likely. Jesus wanted to teach his disciples, but also to give the teachers the chance to recognise their sins and repent.

We don't know what happened to the widow after this incident, but in giving all she had, she demonstrated her faith in God's provision. The poorest among us often have the greatest awareness of their reliance on God.

The learned teachers, by contrast, were putting their faith in their own abilities, manipulating others in order to fill their coffers and caring about their own security more than God's work.

Where do you think you sit on the spectrum? Are you more like the poor widow, giving her all to the Lord? Or like the teachers, seeking honour and ensuring you get what you're owed?

> 'All these people gave their gifts out of their wealth; but she out of her poverty put in all she had to live on.'
>
> **Luke 21:4**

RESPOND

Most of us are much more like the teachers of the law than the widow. Ask God to show you where you are clinging to position, possessions or power instead of surrendering it all to him.

*Judson W Van DeVenter (1855–1939), 'I Surrender All'

Bible in a year: Deuteronomy 25,26; Romans 6

Tuesday 28 March
Luke 21:5–24

Killed... but not harmed

PREPARE

As you come to today's reading, give God the things that are on your mind. Commit them to his safe keeping so you can focus on his Word.

READ

Luke 21:5–24

EXPLORE

A couple of days ago we thought about what it means to live in the light of our future resurrection. This passage gives one 'worked example'.

Look at verses 16–18. Jesus predicted what many of his followers, both soon after his ascension and up to the present day, would face: rejection, betrayal, hatred, persecution. Some would be killed for their faith, but even to those, Jesus promises, 'But not a hair of your head will perish' (v 18). We may lose our lives on this earth, but this earth isn't all there is. It isn't the real thing. When we stand before the Lord in glory, we will find that not a single hair has been harmed, no matter what we have suffered.

And Jesus teaches us how to approach such persecutions: 'Make up your mind not to worry beforehand how you will defend yourselves' (v 14). This isn't just saying 'don't worry about tomorrow's problems today', but '*decide* today that you're not going to worry about your problems tomorrow'! How amazing! We can stop future anxiety now by deciding to trust God to keep his promises.

> '... before all this, they will seize you and persecute you. They will ... put you in prison, and you will be brought before kings and governors, and all on account of my name.'
>
> **Luke 21:12**

RESPOND

There is much to worry about in the world. This passage reminds us that God knows about it all and we can trust him even when things seem to go wrong. Ask him to help you cast all your anxieties on him (1 Peter 5:7).

Bible in a year: Deuteronomy 27,28; Romans 7

Wednesday 29 March

Luke 21:25–38

Standing tall to the end

PREPARE

Our physical posture both reflects and affects our mental and emotional state. If you can, roll your shoulders back, raise your head, and lift your eyes towards heaven as you ask God to speak to you today.

READ

Luke 21:25–38

EXPLORE

This is a continuation of yesterday's passage, with Jesus warning his hearers of all the terrors that would come before this world passes away. Unfortunately, believers through the ages have often been more concerned with interpreting the signs than with responding in the way Jesus told us to. Each new war, each new totalitarian regime, each new natural disaster sparks fraught debate about whether or not we are in the end times.

Jesus gives us three things we should do in the light of these warnings. First, he gives us the attitude with which believers should face the future: standing tall, with our heads held high, in confident assurance of our redemption (v 28). Second, we must be careful not to get too wrapped up in either the anxieties or the pleasures of this world (v 34). And finally, we are to watch and pray, so we are ready when the time comes (v 36).

Jesus did not try to pretend that we will never suffer, but he assured us that as children of God we need not live in fear, for our future is secure.

'When these things begin to take place, stand up and lift up your heads, because your redemption is drawing near.'

Luke 21:28

RESPOND

Ask the Lord to fill you with this confident hope in him. It may not happen in a moment, but trust him to strengthen you more each day as you fix your eyes on him.

Bible in a year: Deuteronomy 29,30; Psalm 36

Thursday 30 March
Luke 22:1–13

Just as Jesus had told them

PREPARE

Where have you seen God's faithfulness in your life or others' lives? Thank him that he is trustworthy and ask him to increase your faith that his other promises will be fulfilled.

READ

Luke 22:1–13

EXPLORE

This is the second time in our readings in Luke that we have seen Jesus send his disciples with mysterious instructions to do things he needs. Some people think that perhaps Jesus had arranged it all in advance with the donkey's owner and the owner of the house. In the story in chapter 19, that is possible, but it is very hard to imagine him organising today's activities. How would you arrange for a man to be walking through the right part of town with a water jar (usually a woman's task) at the perfect moment – all with no mobile phone?!

It is no harder to believe that he knew the actions and the heart of the man with the jar than that he healed the sick and raised the dead! He knew the man would be willing to share his home, and he knew when he would be popping out for water, so he sent the disciples at just the right time.

His disciples knew him well enough not to argue, but to simply obey and do all that he told them to. Are we willing to do the same?

> He replied, 'As you enter the city, a man carrying a jar of water will meet you. Follow him to the house that he enters.'
>
> **Luke 22:10**

RESPOND

How does it make you feel to think that God knows your every thought and action before you do? It is a great mystery, but one that should cause us to be honest in prayer, since he knows anyway.

Bible in a year: Deuteronomy 31,32; Romans 8

Friday 31 March

Luke 22:14–23

Out with the old...

PREPARE

Eating together is an important part of the life of the church. Thank God for the gift of food and consider inviting someone round for a meal soon.

READ

Luke 22:14–23

EXPLORE

It is very clear in today's reading that Jesus knew his time was at hand (vs 15,16). He had eagerly anticipated this special meal that marked the end of an era – not just in his life on earth, but for all those who believe in him.

The Passover meal was instituted in Exodus 12 as a meal of thanksgiving for God's deliverance of his people from Egypt. But at this celebration, Jesus revealed the beginning of a new covenant, marked by a new feast.

In the old feast, a perfect lamb was sacrificed on behalf of the people. Its blood was poured out and painted on the doorposts. Those who came under this symbolic 'covering' of the blood of the lamb would be saved from destruction (Exodus 12:22,23).

Now Jesus was saying the old covenant was passing away, to be replaced by a new and better one (v 20). This one would be made in his own blood and would be open to everyone who believed in him. We who accept Christ come under the protective covering of his blood, and we celebrate that through the new 'feast' of Communion.

... after the supper he took the cup, saying, 'This cup is the new covenant in my blood, which is poured out for you.'

Luke 22:20

RESPOND

'Father God, thank you for sending your Son as our perfect sacrifice. Lord Jesus, thank you for taking on flesh, being broken and poured out for us. Holy Spirit, thank you for empowering us to accept this gift of salvation.'

Bible in a year: Deuteronomy 33,34; Romans 9